Remembrances
of the
Forgotten War

Also by Donald K. Chung

The Three Day Promise

Remembrances of the Forgotten War

A Korean American War Veteran's Journeys for Freedom

Donald K. Chung, M.D.

Introduction by
General William C. Westmoreland, USA (Ret)

Pacifica Press

Manufactured in the United States of America

Cover design by Moody Graphics, Gladstone, Missouri
Drawings by Myung-su Shin

Library of Congress Cataloging-in-Publication Data

Chung, Donald K.
    Remembrances of the forgotten war : a Korean
American war veteran's journeys for freedom / Donald K.
Chung ; introduction by General William C. Westmoreland.
    216 p.
    ISBN 0-935553-10-X: 20.00 U.S.
    1. Chung, Donald K.–Journeys–Korea (North).
2. Korean American physicians–Biography. 3. Family
reunions–Korea (North). 4. Korea (North)–Descriptions.
and travel.   I. Title.
R154-C334A3   1995
951.904'2'092–dc20
[B]   95-13354
                                                            CIP

For my family—
Young-ja, Richard, and Alexander

INTRODUCTION

Dear Dr. Chung:

I have received your letter and a draft of your book *Remembrances of the Forgotten War.* Your story is an interesting one, and well expressed. It is my pleasure to endorse it as a worthy account of the trial, challenges, and heroic success of a worthy Korean patriot–now a worthy American citizen.

Your generous donation of profits from the sale of your book is appreciated by me and I believe most, if not all, of the American veterans of the war.

The Korea/Vietnam Memorial National Education Center in Bethlehem, Pennsylvania, made possible by your contributions, will honor the many American men and women who served their country–many giving their lives–during the wars in Korea and Vietnam.

Your book and your generosity will be remembered by the many citizens who will visit the center in the future, and at the same time remind them of the sacrifices that have been made by you and many.

WILLIAM CHILDS WESTMORELAND
General, United States Army, Retired

Dear Dr. Chung:

On behalf of the Korea/Vietnam Memorial National
Education Center (KVMNEC), please accept our sincere
thanks and appreciation for your generous donation of all
profits from the sale of your book *Remembrances of the
Forgotten War* to the KVMNEC.

Your contribution will play a significant role in
establishing the Korean/Vietnam Memorial National
Education Center, whose goal is to create and operate a
Living Memorial to honor those brave men and women
who sacrificed   so much for our freedom and peace in the
Korean and Vietnam wars.

As a senior officer who served as the commander of
the 2d Battalion, 15th Infantry Regiment, 3d Infantry
Division, in the Korean War, I was deeply moved by
reading your manuscript, which vividly described painful
accounts of the war, separation of millions of Korean people
from their loved ones for the past forty-five years. I was
touched by reading many quotes from letters which you
have received from all over the world, including Korean
War veterans, their families, many Koreans who are still
separated from their loved ones in North Korea, and those
who lost their loved ones in the war.

Dr. Chung, through your generous support, you are
helping us to honor the sixteen million American men and
women who served our country during the wars in Korea
and Vietnam, and especially the 115,000 who were killed or
remain missing in action.

On April 18, 1994, a KVMNEC delegation went to
Korea to brief President Kim Young-sam about KVMNEC.
In fact, President Kim strongly endorsed our project and
stated, "This project is long overdue."

We must understand that the Cold War did not simply end–it was won. History will show us that the Cold War was won by our fighting men and women in Korea, Vietnam, and in the Gulf War. As citizens of the free world, we cannot forget our heroic troops' sacrifices and contributions to the security of our nations and to freedom and democracy around the world. KVMNEC will help keep alive the memory of all veterans who fought and served in Korea and Vietnam. KVMNEC will house a research center which will be the only such comprehensive depository in the world. There, one will find documents, films, and videotapes about the Korean and Vietnam Wars.

Some of the significant features of the Center will include: the "Korean War Trail," which will display an outdoor replica of the Korean peninsula, with a walking trail   of twenty historic battle sites of the Korean War; the "Vietnam War Trail," which will display an outdoor replica of Vietnam, with a walking trail of twenty historic battle sites of the Vietnam War; and computerized, videotaped biographical data of the veterans of the Korean and Vietnam Wars.

Remembrances of the Forgotten War is a unique contribution to the history of the Korean War, and it is also a success story of a Korean American in the United States. I recommend Dr. Chung's book to all citizens who love freedom and especially to veterans who served in the Korean and Vietnam wars.

Thank you again for your unselfish generosity to KVMNEC. You will be remembered by millions who will visit the center for years to come.

JOHN K. SINGLAUB
Major General, United States Army, Retired
Honorary Vice Chairman
Korea/Vietnam Memorial National Education Center

PROLOGUE
Dong-kyu's Story
A Summary of The Three Day Promise

Chung Dong-kyu was born in the tiny Korean farming village of Taehyang, near the far-northern town of Chu-ul, on February 6, 1932. His parents, Chung Bong-chun and Kim Ki-bok, were country people in their late twenties, who had spent their entire lives under Japanese rule. Two years after the birth of his only son (there were also three daughters), the elder Chung, who was twenty-eight years old at the time and modestly educated, left Taehyang to seek a better life. He ended up in Harbin, Manchuria, where he found work with the Japanese occupation government as a clerk in the city district attorney's office. The family soon joined him and established a household in the extremely cosmopolitan city, with its large Manchurian, Chinese, Japanese, Korean, and even White Russian populations. One price the son had to pay for his father's good fortune in finding a comfortable, well-paying government job in Harbin was the submergence of his Korean identity. When he started school, Chung Dong-kyu was given a Japanese name and taught only in the

Japanese language. His Korean ways were not lost, but they were actively suppressed.

Chung Bong-chun was not an exemplary father. Apart from being naturally reticent with his children, he used his position in the district attorney's office to extract bribes from Korean families whose members had been caught in the lucrative smuggling trade between Manchuria, Korea, and Japan. He also kept a concubine. While in the Asia of the time these were hardly unique or even egregious offenses, the elder Chung also turned out to be a grievously selfish man. He not only flaunted his concubine, he spent nearly all his earnings on her while keeping his natural family in the least acceptable circumstances. One result of this cruel way of life was the turning of the son toward the mother. Young Dong-kyu had feelings for his father, the result of traditional Asian teachings, but his real love and his real anchor in life was his mother, Kim Ki-bok.

In midsummer 1945, thirteen-year-old Chung Dong-kyu came down with a sudden and nearly fatal case of appendicitis. The ministrations of a Chinese herbalist nearly killed the boy, and it was almost too late when his mother rushed him to a Western-style hospital, where a Japanese physician operated to remove the by-then burst appendix and repair all the damage. Young Dong-kyu, who was awake and alert throughout the procedure, found wonder once the fear subsided. During a slow but complete recovery, Dong-kyu's fascination with Western-style medicine turned into a quest. He had no idea how he might become a physician, but he was determined to do so.

Dong-kyu was still in the hospital, recovering from his surgery, when the Japanese staff suddenly evacuated the city. It was August 11, 1945; the atomic bombs had been dropped, and Japan was about to surrender to the Allies. It was the first news the family had that Japan had suffered a setback in the war, much less a crushing defeat.

Japan acceded to Allied surrender terms on August 15, 1945, and the city of Harbin came under Soviet military occupation within a matter of days. Shortly, the Soviet troops ran amok in Harbin, and a simple house check degenerated into the brutal gang rape of Dong-kyu's eldest sister, Moon-hee—right before Dong-kyu's eyes. Unarmed and still too weak to act, the teenager suffered grievous guilt. It also separated him yet that much more from his father, who was hiding out at the home of his concubine rather than with his family.

Shortly after the rape, the mother's home was visited by a Korean Communist who was working with the Soviet occupiers, tracking down Koreans who had worked for the Japanese. Despite her husband's awful treatment of his family, Kim Ki-bok paid the man a bribe in order to have Chung Bong-chun's name removed from the fatal list. The bribe the man demanded, and won, was a night with Moon-hee, the elder daughter who had been raped a few days earlier by Soviet troops. Although the family was revolted beyond words, the mother and daughter nevertheless saved the life of their errant husband and father. But the cost was the loss of Moon-hee's spirit. For the rest of her time in Harbin, the comely young woman masqueraded as a boy.

In September 1945, Chung Bong-chun fled Harbin. He told the family he would try to reach Seoul, whereupon he would send for them. But only a few days later, a Korean in the employ of the Soviets organized a train journey to repatriate Koreans from Harbin to their homeland. Kim Ki-bok jumped at the opportunity, and the family alighted in Chu-ul, within miles of home. The journey was the least-painful experience to befall the mother and her children since Dong-kyu's nearly fatal illness, and it began a period of calm and relative happiness that lasted nearly five years. However, the scars accrued by Dong-kyu from the harrowing months of August and September 1945 would haunt him for a lifetime and, by the way, shape for him a destiny from which he could not backtrack.

Within a short time of its arrival from Harbin, the family settled into an old house in Chu-ul. Dong-kyu began making friends, and at school he learned to read and write in the Korean language. For the moment, the only sour note was the father's relationship with a new concubine.

At the same time Harbin and the rest of Manchuria had been occupied by Soviet troops, the northern half of Korea, down to the 38th Parallel, had also been taken under Soviet domination. Backed by the guns of the occupation forces, Korean Communists installed themselves in power throughout the land and began an aggressive transformation of the country. In short order, Dong-kyu's favorite uncle was tried by a "people's court," because he had been a policeman serving the Japanese. He was sentenced to hard labor in a coal mine. Other changes were also afoot, but most of them were mild and actually had a positive impact upon a people who had been brutally ruled by Japanese outsiders for more than a generation.

One of the benefits the Communists sought to implement was a fine medical-delivery structure. Koreans had been systematically denied medical educations under the Japanese, so there were few Korean physicians in the nation in 1946. One early solution was the selection and training of medical practitioners—something more than a nurse but still less than a doctor. The idea was to provide masses of them. A medical-technical high school was established in the provincial capital of Chongjin, and a recruitment drive was instituted in June 1946.

Fueled by memories of his emergency appendectomy only a year earlier, Chung Dong-kyu decided to apply for a place at the three-year medical-technical high school, which was only a few hours' journey from his home in Chu-ul. He was not an especially good student, but he had a fierce desire to practice the type of Western-style medicine that would be taught there. Despite his many handicaps–Korean was pretty much his second language, and he had never been a high achiever–Dong-kyu was one of just sixty students accepted for the training program's first class.

In September 1948, after two years in operation, the medical-technical high school in Chongjin was reaccredited and upgraded to a full-fledged medical college, one of three in Soviet-occupied northern Korea. Though he was still only sixteen, Chung Dong-kyu took the college entrance exam, which he passed as the freshman class's youngest member. Virtually overnight, the training program improved in every conceivable way, from equipment to textbooks to qualified teaching doctors. Something also changed in Dong-kyu, who went from being merely a good student to being a superior student; he maintained the highest possible grade-point average in every course except inorganic chemistry.

The only major ongoing problem Dong-kyu encountered during his two years at the medical-technical high school and his first two years at the medical college was his virtual isolation from his family during the long months when school was in session. He went home whenever he could, but there was an edge of depression that came with such journeys. Dong-kyu's father, who was by then a Communist Party functionary, continued to flaunt his relationship with his concubine, and Dong-kyu's mother continued to suffer in silence. Also, Moon-hee endured two brief and troubled marriages before leaving the region to become a guard at a prison for women. Eventually, the perpetually missing father absented himself all the way to Pyongyang, the national capital, to take up a bureaucratic political post.

During the nearly five years between the end of the war and Dong-kyu's second year in medical college, life in northern Korea became harsher. Supported by Soviet occupation troops, Korean Communists led by Kim Il-sung took over the entire government apparatus, down to the lowest levels of community life. There were good things to be credited to the regime, such as the expanded medical program that was being built up, but political and social repression became more severe and widespread with each passing month. (In many ways, daily life in northern Korea–which became the Democratic People's Republic of Korea on September 9, 1948– followed a Stalinist Russian model more than the traditional Korean model everyone had hoped it might.)

At the start of Dong-kyu's sophomore year at the medical college, the students were more or less inducted into the new national army, and military indoctrination and training became part of the daily curriculum. During the spring of 1950, all the medical students were given a special course in the classification and treatment of war wounds, and then all were offered commissions as officer-doctors in the North Korean People's Army. It was only then that Chung Dong-kyu finally noticed that the entire nation was in the midst of becoming an armed camp.

At first, the Chongjin Medical College, and Chung Dong-kyu in particular, were barely affected by the onset of the Korean War. From June 25–the date of North Korea's invasion of the south–the students and faculty carried on almost as they had in the prior years of peace. There was an upsurge in patriotic speeches and reports, but nothing more happened at the school for three weeks. As far as the students and most North Koreans were concerned, their peaceful nation had been attacked, and their brave army had advanced deep into South Korea during the course of a purely reactive counterattack.

In mid-July, the medical college's junior class (there was no senior class yet) was drafted en masse into the North Korean army. And two weeks later, just before the end of July, the port of Chongjin was attacked by United States Air Force heavy bombers. As the bombers flew away, all of the medical students were given aid packs and rushed to the areas of devastation. And so Chung Dong-kyu had his first encounter with applied medical science. The experience was nearly overwhelming for the young man. The neat orderliness of the school examining rooms and operating theaters was nowhere to be found. There was only chaos. He administered aid—mostly in the form of morphine to victims trapped in the rubble of collapsed buildings—and carried on in a daze of automatic response at the most basic instinctual level.

Thereafter, the days of learning were often punctuated by the sound of air-raid sirens and even the occasional bombing attack on Chongjin, which was one of North Korea's major ports and industrial centers. In time, classes were suspended completely so the medical students could devote all their time to treating the hospital's share of North Korea's many thousands of war wounded. From then on, each new air-raid warning meant the suspension of treatment so all the casualties could be rushed to caves in a mountainside two miles away. In early September, United Nations warships began pounding the city from uncontested stations offshore. The casualty toll rose and the quality of treatment plummeted, but Dong-kyu and his fellow medical students carried on, though almost in a daze of fragmented time delimited less by the passage of days than the rising count of bombardments.

In late September 1950, the Chongjin Medical College was closed, and the students were dispersed to hospitals and clinics throughout the country. Dong-kyu was assigned to the regional hospital at Chu-ul, so he was able to move back in with his mother and younger sister, June-hee, who still remained at home.

The sojourn at the Chu-ul hospital lasted only a week, and then Dong-kyu received his call-up notice to the army. Despite witnessing ample horror in Chongjin, the extremity of the war had not set in on the young man until that moment. He was eighteen and only half-trained, but cir-cumstances had degenerated to the point where he was considered qualified to serve as a full-fledged army physician.

That evening, when Kim Ki-bok heard that her son had been called to the army, the abused wife acted with a speed and resolution Dong-kyu had until then only hoped she had in her reservoir of powers. She immediately packed her son a bag of clothing and food and led him into the night to Taehyang, the family seat, where he was hidden in a barn for the night and then moved to the innards of a large clay pot. And there he hid for nearly seven weeks, until Taehyang was captured by Republic of Korea–South Korean–soldiers on November 21, 1950.

Had he been captured by his "own" soldiers while hiding out, Chung Dong-kyu would have been executed out of hand. He remained in hiding for four more days, to give his mother time to see how things were going under the southerners; then she turned him loose into an entirely new atmosphere. After one more day in Taehyang, he returned to Chu-ul and reopened the city hospital with the help of two nurses.

On the very first day on the job at Chu-ul, Dong-kyu was called to the site of a terrible massacre in the nearby moun-tains. The frozen, mutilated corpses of several dozen women had been discovered beneath the snow; all had been executed by retreating North Korean security police after it was dis-covered that they had been aiding loved ones who had staged a brief insurrection in a nearby town. One of the women was Dong-kyu's aunt. In short order, the family also learned that Dong-kyu's uncle, who had been sentenced to hard labor in a coal mine in 1946 for working as a Japanese military police-man, had recently been executed along with hundreds of other miner-prisoners when their guards were forced to flee ahead of liberating United Nations troops. In only a few days, many more stories of atrocities committed by Communist troops and police poured in.

◆

The new regime lasted barely a week. Suddenly, on December 2, 1950, the southern troops began pulling out of the area. Rumors spread that hundreds of thousands of Chinese Communist troops had invaded Korea from Manchuria and that they were overwhelming American and South Korean troops along the entire front. However, a South Korean soldier assured Dong-kyu that this was merely a three-day tactical retreat to allow United Nations forces to mass for a counter-counterattack.

Dong-kyu reached his own decision this time, perhaps the first adult decision he had ever made. Fearful of being captured by the oncoming Communist troops, he decided to go south with the southerners. He promised his mother that when they returned in three days, he would return with them. Reluctantly agreeing, Kim Ki-bok once again packed a small parcel of food and clothing for her only son. As the young man prepared to leave, the mother's instincts gave way; for the only time he could remember, she broke down to beseech him to come home as soon as possible, to remain away from her for the shortest amount of time he could. Once again, he promised to return with the southern troops in only three days. And then he fled into the night with throngs of other northerners accompanying the southern army's rearguard.

The long retreat before the oncoming Chinese army lasted more than a week. Along the way, thousands of ill-prepared civilians froze to death in the snow or starved. On the journey, Chung Dong-kyu caught a glimpse of his father, who had briefly returned to Chu-ul with the retreating North Korean troops. That glimpse was the last time any member of the family saw Chung Bong-chun.

The momentum of Dong-kyu's retreat alongside the southern troops carried him—and tens of thousands of other refugees—to the port of Songjin, one of two eastern ports through which the southern and United Nations troops were being evacuated. Though mindful of his promise to return to

Chu-ul, Dong-kyu nevertheless took the opportunity before him and boarded one of the ships carrying troops and civilians to the south.

As soon as the ship arrived at a small southern port and Dong-kyu disembarked with a group of young northern men, he was inducted straight into the Republic of Korea Army. No one asked if he had any special talents or training—his medical training was completely overlooked. On the spot, he was made an infantry reconnaissance scout because his northern accent was considered an invaluable asset for such an assignment.

Chung Dong-kyu served honorably, faithfully, and in some cases with exceptional bravery throughout the remainder of the Korean War. He learned to be a good soldier, and he rose steadily to the rank of sergeant, as much a testament to his mere survival as to his budding leadership skills. On rare occasions, he encountered former friends and classmates from the north who, like him, had been inducted or dragooned into the southern army. There were endless reminders for the young soldier that he was fighting for a home far from home, kept by a fratricidal war from fulfilling his promise to his mother, his promise to return to her side.

Toward the end of the war, after looking around and seeing that more than half of his original comrades from the north (130 of 156) had been killed or wounded, and fearing that his number on the battlefield was long past due coming up, Sergeant Chung Dong-kyu contacted a cousin who was serving as a high-ranking intelligence officer in the southern army. The cousin pulled a few strings and had Dong-kyu transferred to his staff. A few weeks after that, the cousin had the fully qualified combat scout transferred to a medical battalion to serve as a hospital orderly. (During his only leave in the entire war, Dong-kyu had accidentally discovered that many of his former medical-school colleagues had been inducted as doctors or physicians' assistants into the southern army—or even allowed to attend southern medical schools—after coming south.)

When the Korean armistice was signed in July 1953, Sergeant Chung Dong-kyu reenlisted. At the time, he was despondent over news that many Republic of Korea Army combat veterans from the north—himself included—were being denied veterans' educational benefits. Northerners he knew who had not served as long nor even in combat units were granted such rights, and several of his medical-school classmates were continuing their educations in southern schools. But he was given no benefits whatsoever, because his induction directly into the army upon reaching the south had prevented him from acquiring the narrow qualifications required to obtain the postwar benefit. The army's only concession to his medical training in the north was allowing him to continue to serve as a hospital orderly. However, fortunately, this led to a temporary training assignment at a U.S. Army field hospital.

The duty at the American hospital—his first protracted exposure to Americans—changed Sergeant 1st Class Chung's view of the world. Comparing the modern American *field* facility with permanent "advanced" hospitals in both the north and south made the orderly's mind hum with the possibilities—and it permanently changed his life. His persistent despondency lifted during this temporary posting, and Dong-kyu made vague plans to complete his medical degree—somehow—just so he could practice medicine in the wonderful, far-off country that gave its field soldiers better medical care than could be provided by the South Korean government to its citizens in any of the south's finest hospitals.

When Sergeant 1st Class Chung Dong-kyu mustered out of the Republic of Korea Army in July 1956, he had nothing except the clothing on his back—an army uniform he had dyed black. There was no pension and no benefits to show for his nearly six years of loyal service. There were no jobs, either, for the former soldier, and he didn't have enough capital even to become a street peddler. But Dong-kyu's luck returned within a month. At a public swimming pool in Seoul, he ran into a former professor from Chongjin. When the doctor heard Dong-kyu's story, he hired the former student on the spot to work—and even live—at his thriving private clinic. As soon as the new employee was settled in, the talented doctor resumed his role as teacher; Dong-kyu went back to medical school as the former professor's only student, and all his long-suppressed hopes were kindled anew.

In the spring of 1957, Soo-do Medical College, a women's school, opened its enrollment to transfer students and men. At the urging of his benefactor, who taught there, Dong-kyu applied. Following an entrance examination—his first real academic test in more than six years—he was accepted as a probationary student in the sophomore class. But an even bigger hurdle faced him: Tuition was more than $6,000 per year, far more than he supposed he could earn while attending classes.

All things considered, Chung Dong-kyu had been a very lucky boy and man. Though the product of an unhappy union, he had been bolstered through most of his life by the unequivocal love of his mother. Though his early formal education had taken place entirely in a foreign language (Japanese), his native intellect had cleared a place for him in the higher reaches of his nation's educational system. Though he had known more than his share of danger and peril, he had escaped death and even injury while most of his comrades had died. Faced with abject poverty at a crucial moment in life, he had blundered into an old admirer, who had given him a job, a place to live, and vital support in reembarking upon his life's desire: a Western-style medical education.

But now Dong-kyu's life took a new turn. He would need his luck, to be sure, but he would henceforth rely mainly upon an iron will to succeed, upon hard work and more hard work, and upon utter devotion to his cause–the attainment of a superior education in his chosen field. With no hope of earning the tuition, Dong-kyu embarked upon a bold plan; he contacted every former colleague he could track down–old army buddies and former classmates and friends from the north. Each was asked to *invest* in Dong-kyu's medical education, or at least float a loan. The journey through most of South Korea was nearly an epic in itself, and the chore was doubly hard because so many of the people he knew lived in straitened circumstances. But in the end, Dong-kyu returned to Seoul with slightly more money than he needed for his first year's tuition.

Classes began on April 1, 1957. Fortunately, though he was extremely rusty, Dong-kyu's sophomore curriculum at Soo-do Medical College was largely a repeat of his sophomore training at Chongjin. He was able to ease back into the academic life by repeating courses in which he had earlier excelled. This was crucial to his success, for the attainment of full acceptance to the course hinged upon his academic standing at the end of the first semester. If he did well, he could stay; if not, he would be dismissed. The only problem was that most medical terms at Soo-do were rendered in English, and not the Russian Dong-kyu had learned at Chongjin. Also, he had not borrowed enough money to purchase the required medical texts. He made up both deficits by transcribing the texts by hand–learning the English terms as he went–but that meant long hours of work at night, which in turn meant not sleeping adequately. He also continued to earn his room and board by working at the clinic of his former Chongjin professor.

The hard work and privation paid off; Dong-kyu scored such high grades in the first-semester finals that he received a scholarship amounting to half his junior-year tuition. This success led to a lucrative offer from an older classmate: In return for helping the classmate with his studies, Dong-kyu was taken in as a boarder and given a stipend somewhat larger than his clinic salary. In sum, he would be able to devote less time to earning his keep and more time to study and rest.

That people thought well of Dong-kyu was nowhere better exemplified than in what happened next. He spent the summer break working at the newly opened clinic of a dear northern friend who had just graduated from a southern medical school. At the end of the summer, the friend gave Dong-kyu the cash he needed to cover the portion of junior-year tuition not covered by the scholarship. It was a bequest made at great sacrifice to his friend and his friend's family, and it was sweeter yet because Dong-kyu had in no way asked that it be made.

By remaining at the top of his class, Dong-kyu continued to receive his scholarship, and he used his notoriety as a superior student to earn the rest by translating medical texts for other students and, eventually, writing and publishing two medical-school workbooks. He was actually quite successful as an entrepreneur and was thus able to afford decent clothes and the occasional treat, even a monthly haircut. He did even better during his senior year, when many medical students retained him as a tutor. One of the tutorial students did so well in his tests that he bought Dong-kyu a Western-style suit, Dong-kyu's first. And it was that good suit that Dong-kyu was wearing when, on March 21, 1960, he finally became entitled to be addressed as *Doctor* Chung Dong-kyu.

With the hurdle of medical school behind him, Dong-kyu faced his next self-imposed quest. It was not enough merely to graduate from medical school, not even when he did so at the top of his class. He now had to obtain certification as a physician by acquiring an internship post at a qualified hospital. And here an old dream came into play. Dong-kyu had been intensely interested in going to America from the time he had been temporarily posted to the U.S. Army field hospital after the end of the Korean War. He had fallen in love with Americans and the idea of becoming one. His goal upon entering Soo-do Medical College had been to make his way after graduation to the land of that lavishly appointed field hospital—for if that was the way America treated its soldiers in the field, Dong-kyu simply had to see how a nation that enjoyed such immense wealth treated its civilians.

The airfare was too high, and he had not heard back from the American programs to which he had applied. He took an unpaid internship at the Soo-do Medical College Hospital and earned living expenses and money toward his fare from several medical clinics in Seoul. Along the way, he passed the government medical boards and thus became a certified physician. During this period, he firmed up his plan to become a cardiologist so he could emulate his favorite professor at Soo-do. When he completed his internship, he was accepted as a cardiology resident. But, although two years passed without a word from any of the American hospitals, his desire to go to the United States never waned.

In 1962, Dr. Chung passed an American entrance examination for the Educational Council for Foreign Medical Graduates and by then he had saved enough money to fly to the United States and live there for several months, looking for an opportunity. Then he was accepted as an intern at the Missouri Baptist Hospital in St. Louis. Going to America meant regressing in status from second-year cardiology resident to rotating intern, but it was a step that had to be taken on the road to certification in the United States.

And so it went. Dong-kyu flew to St. Louis in September 1962 and went straight to work on his new life. In due course, he earned his certification as a cardiologist, got married, became an American citizen, fathered two sons, and generally became the very embodiment of the American Dream. And yet, for all that success and fulfillment, not a day goes by without his taking time to remember his humble origins, his mother and the family he left behind, the privations of war, his divided homeland, the burden of attaining a fine education–and the names and faces of all the people who helped him achieve goals that often seemed remote and un- attainable. Not a day goes by without his thanking each of them, for he knows in his heart that without any single one of them he could have stumbled, could have fallen short. His life's work has always been healing, but now he adds to that the never-ending task of remembering.

PART I

The Three Day Promise Fulfilled

Chapter 1

Life was good to me. Over the years, I obtained all the material possessions an American man could desire. My family gave me joy and pride. I was liked and respected by my patients and friends. I had standing in my community.

But something remained elusively beyond my grasp. I knew all along what it was, but it took the trauma of turning fifty years old to draw it into the open. I had been an unworthy son; I had not done enough with my money and my standing to return to my family in North Korea—for a visit, for a reunion, for a homecoming.

Throughout the second half of 1982, I made inquiries. These were largely through the Korean community in Canada, which because of a different political climate had better ties with North Korea. I made little progress at first—I was one of many thousands of refugees attempting to gain news from and access to North Korea. But I did inch forward.

On May 17, 1983, my inquiries brought a crushing response: My mother had passed away several years earlier.

Two of my three sisters, however, had been located; I still had living ties to my homeland.

Within a few weeks, I was granted permission to visit North Korea, and I received a letter from Moon-hee, my eldest sister, on June 24, just two weeks before my planned departure. She told me I had nine nephews and four nieces, and that my other two sisters, Ok-bong and Jung-hee, were well. I received great joy from this news, but I also grieved deeply for having done my duty too late to see my mother again. I also learned from Moon-hee's letter that my father had never been heard from after he left home the same time as I had, in December 1950. I had seen him one last time on the road to freedom, in the snow, but no one had seen him since.

I left for Beijing, China, on July 3, 1983, and arrived on July 4. I gave a lecture at the Beijing Medical College on the morning of the fifth, and traveled to Pyongyang that afternoon. Minutes after landing, I met Ok-bong and Jung-hee for the first time in nearly thirty-three years. It was a moment too long in coming, though I doubt there was any way I could have made it happen much earlier than it did, because of politics and fear.

This was no ordinary visit, like a reunion among family members in the free world. This was a political event and it was tightly controlled in every aspect. We were taken firmly in tow by a polite but quite immovable official guide, who would be with me almost every moment of my stay in North Korea.

It was obvious at the outset that North Korea was not a happy land, nor were North Koreans happy people. They appeared well looked-after, but they were lifeless and wooden as far as I could see. Even my sisters were guarded and distant. They said all the right things to put me at my ease, but there was that official guide, and so all the right things were said as a matter of form to please the extra set of ears. It was the things that were *not* said that I longed to hear; it was the warmth that was not shared that I longed to feel.

In the days following my arrival, I was given the grand tour of Pyongyang. There I was told what I must see, what I must think, what I must know. It was a political tour, pure and simple. I was not aware of its exact purpose, but I well knew that an attempt was being made to win my mind, or at least alter my outlook. I would not have been allowed to set foot inside the country if they did not think they could manipulate my point of view. I was circumspect. I had my own reasons for being there and I was willing to endure the charade to meet my own goals.

The official grand tour lasted four days. Then I was allowed to travel—with my ubiquitous guide—to Ok-bong's home, which was far to the northeast in the town of Myongchun. We passed through Songjin, the port from which I had departed North Korea in December 1950. And we left the train at Kilchu, a large town I had tramped through on my final journey from my home in Chu-ul to Songjin.

Among those awaiting me in Kilchu was my beloved eldest sister, Moon-hee. I knew it was her before she even saw me. A great warmth filled my heart as we embraced, for she was only slightly less a mother to me than our mother had been. But then the sadness returned, for she was not quite my mother. These enormous tides of joy mixed with despair could well have pulled me apart. I also realized how close we were to the last place I had seen our father, and that nearly ripped me in two.

That afternoon I completed my quest. After eating lunch at Ok-bong's house, we went to the cemetery. And there I had my tearful reunion with the kind, simple woman who had given me life.

In an oval grave about ten feet in diameter, Mother awaited me. There was about a half-inch of lush, well-tended green grass growing over her. At one end of the oval was a

tiny concrete marker about three feet high by one foot on
each side; upon it were inscribed Korean hangul characters
bearing the name, "Kim Ki-bok." To the right of Mother's
name were the dates, "July 5, 1904—September 19, 1979."
More characters to the left of the name bore a statement
that staggered me: "Owner of Grave: Chung Dong-kyu."

I have never felt a deeper, more profound sorrow in my
entire life. I fell to my knees and clasped the stone to my
chest, crying and whimpering, "Mother! I could not keep The
Promise. I could not return to you in three days. But I am
back now, beside you."

The tears flowing from my eyes. The warmth of the sun.
The distant odor of cultivated soil. The rustling of a light
breeze through trees overhead. The softness of the grass car-
pet beneath my knees. The sun-warmed stone touching my
arms and chest and cheeks. Mother's ethereal presence. The
realization that I was as close to my beginnings as I would
ever be again. The seeming futility of my lifelong dreams.

I don't know which of these things, or what combination,
caused it, but I opened the great wound in my soul and flushed
out the disease that had been within me. I cleansed the essence of my being as I knelt over the woman who had made me.

"I am back, Mother. Back beside you. There has not been
a moment in all these thirty-three years that you were not
with me. The thought of you gave me the courage to survive
and to go on, to become a man you would have been proud to
call 'Son.' You were there, Mother, leading me on, pulling me
onward, whenever I fell into despair, whenever I entered the
valley of the shadow. We have been apart, Mother, and we
will never meet again in this life. But you have been one
with me through my whole life, here with you or gone far
across the seas and beyond the gulf of time. And I know,
Mother, that you felt my presence upon this earth for all
the days you lived among us. I know you feel me now, here
beside you."

I threw back my head and stared into the infinite cap of blue sky. I felt, once again, the gentle summer breeze blowing up from the valley and through the trees. I saw renewal in the distant green fields and in the memory of the young faces of nieces and nephews I had first seen over this day's lunch. And then I told Mother about my life.

I told Mother of my last meeting with Father, of the horrible freezing flight to Songjin, and the yet-more-horrid journey at sea. I told her of dead and dying soldiers and of a years-long fear so profound as to be impossible to share even with my own memory. I told her of the soul-crushing poverty I had faced after setting forth into the world from my safe, dull army sinecure. I told her of my empty-seeming dreams and how I had prevailed over my hideous circumstances through unremitting luck and hard work.

I told Mother of healing lives, which had become the essence of my mission in this world. I told her how each life I saved or made less difficult was a dedication and a rededication to an ethic I had learned at her breast—how I literally evoked a memory of her each time I confronted a new patient.

I had to tell her that I retained a powerful memory of each small thing she had done to ease my transition from infancy to the frontier of adulthood. I had to tell her how profoundly I felt and treasured each tiny sacrifice she had made in my behalf.

"I have two sons of my own now, Mother. They are teenagers, partly Korean and partly American. They are good boys. We live in a nice home, and I make a comfortable living. I am married to a Korean woman from the south. We live in two worlds; we are Korean, but we are also American. I believe we fit in well. But we have not forgotten our culture or the old ways.

"I so wanted to show you proof of my achievements, Mother. I am so sorry I could not have come sooner. I was afraid and I was naive. I was not always a man. Now I have only this grave, this stone, and my memories.

"Oh, how I wish I could have seen your face just one last time before you left us!"

In this way I fulfilled the promise I had made thirty-three years earlier.

Chapter 2

I wrote a long, long letter to my dear second sister, Ok-bong, about three weeks after I returned from my visit to North Korea in July 1983. It was prepared while I was vacationing at my Palm Springs house, and it helped me focus my thoughts about all that I had seen and heard and felt during my trip. The letter also helped me settle my emotions and regain my inner equilibrium.

I had mixed feelings. I was happy to find that my three sisters were alive, and I had visited my mother's grave even though the three-day promise to her had been delayed for thirty-three years. On the other hand, I was extremely sad and disturbed to see my sisters living in miserable circumstances. In fact, their living conditions deeply depressed me, especially when I compared them with the comforts almost any American accepts as commonplace.

In my letter, I described to Ok-bong all that I had seen in North Korea. I did not actually comment on any of it, but I described each facet of the visit in detail. What I did not say in the letter was that I fully comprehended the visit as a political and propaganda tool in the hands of the North Korean government. And I did not say anything about all the places and things I would have liked to see there. For example, I had not spoken with a single North Korean citizen outside of my family about how life really was in the north. The tone and content of my letter were neutral, but the letter was nonetheless taken as a very positive declaration of support by the North Koreans. It dwelled on positive things because that's all I had been allowed to see and experience.

A copy of the letter to Ok-bong was subsequently published in a four-part series by the *New Korea Times* newspaper in Toronto, Canada. The publisher was Chun Chung-lim, who had been the one to locate my family in North Korea and arrange my 1983 home visit. After the appearance of this letter in the newspaper, many North Korean refugees living in the United States and Canada called me for help in locating the families they had left behind. I met many of them to provide details of my experience, and I referred all of them to Mr. Chun for assistance.

According to a letter I eventually received from my baby sister, Jung-hee, my letter to Ok-bong also appeared in *Ro-dong Shin-mun,* the official newspaper of the Workers' Party of North Korea. Jung-hee said that all of my family had read it. The story was also widely introduced at different local Workers' Party meetings throughout the country.

Prior to my 1983 visit, the delivery of mail from my sisters had taken several months, and the letters were invariably sent via the Committee for the Aid of Overseas Nationals of the Democratic People's Republic of Korea, in Pyongyang. Following the visit, however, letters from my sisters were delivered to my office much more quickly than before, usually within three weeks. The envelopes were always stamped at their hometown post offices. And now I could mail the letters to my sisters with their address in North Korea from an ordinary mailbox in Long Beach. I could even send my sisters money orders or cashier's checks, purchased at my bank for special occasions. Once the money arrived in North Korea, the personnel at the Committee would exchange it at the proper rate to a special foreign-exchange currency for use by the family. This special currency could be used only at government foreign-currency stores to buy goods and items not generally available to most ordinary North Korean citizens.

In addition, all of the letters I received before my letter to Ok-bong was published had begun in a stereotypical style, saying, "We are all well and happy by grace of our Great Leader, President Kim Il-sung, and the Dear Leader, Comrade Kim Jong-il . . ." Gradually, following my visit, such routine openings were omitted, and my sisters began to write more and more of their personal feelings. When I realized this, I felt that somehow Koreans living in North Korea and elsewhere had gotten one tiny step closer to one another.

While the first series of letters with my sisters was being exchanged, I finished writing the first draft of my memoir, which I called *The Three Day Promise*. I immediately started to send the manuscript to various publishers and literary agents.

In December 1983, an interview article about my hometown revisit appeared on the front page of the Long Beach daily newspaper, the *Press Telegram*. I received several phone calls and letters from families of Korean War participants who were killed in the war.

Following this initial publicity, I was invited to speak before many different organizations, including churches, service clubs, schools, and Korean War veterans' groups. My memories of the trip were still vivid and fresh, and I used color slides that the North Korean government guide had let me take. The groups to which I spoke were interested, especially because so little was known in the West about any aspect of North Korean life. I concluded each presentation by saying, "I pray to Almighty God to bring reunification soon to my homeland so that more than seventeen million people, including my three sisters, can also enjoy the freedom I enjoy today." My heart was aching for this outcome, but even the thought of unification would be put off for years because of the unique stubbornness of our Korean people, especially our politicians.

Somehow the articles that appeared in the *New Korea Times* and the series of slide presentations gave the North Korean government a positive impression of me. I learned this, in fact, in letters from my sisters, who even called me a "real patriot of our fatherland." That was well and good, but none of this improved living conditions for my sisters.

While my status rose in North Korea, I was perceived as being pro—North Korea by the South Korean government. Apparently, people in the South Korean government were quite worked up about my visit and the sentiments they thought I was expressing. I was constantly watched by their security agents operating in the United States, and members of my wife's family who lived in South Korea were interrogated and watched because of my lectures and articles. Eventually, a few close friends advised me to stop writing articles and giving talks about North Korea. They were afraid that I would be harmed. The most disturbing experience of all was when my wife, Young-ja, came to me in tears and begged me to stop because she felt she would be prevented from ever visiting her family in South Korea again.

Exactly a year after my North Korea visit, I had a call from an FBI agent based in Los Angeles. He wanted to visit me to speak about the trip. When I agreed, two agents came to my office that very day, during the lunch hour. They showed me their FBI badges and asked about the trip. I told them, "I will tell you why I had to go and what they showed me. Please do not interrupt me. I'll be glad to comment if you have any further questions after I finish." They agreed by simply nodding their heads.

Telling the FBI agents my story was an easy task for me; I had already presented this tale more than twenty times in half-hour- and hour-long sessions. As agreed, they did not interrupt me, but I could see their eyes almost became lost when I described with a choking voice my visit to my mother's grave. My lecture lasted exactly forty-five minutes. I concluded by saying, "Thank you for your cooperation and attentiveness. Do you wish to ask any questions?"

One of the two said, "You are really good and observant. We don't have any questions."

He looked over to the other agent as if to ask if he agreed, and then they got up and gave me their business cards. As they were leaving, one of them said, "The only reason we came to see you today is because you are a U.S. citizen, and we have an obligation to protect you and your family. Please call us immediately if anyone from North Korea or South Korea threatens you or tries to harm you." I was extremely relieved, and I reaffirmed my happiness to be a citizen of the wonderful United States of America.

When I went home that evening, I told Young-ja about my reassuring visit from the FBI and that I was going to continue giving lectures and writing articles. After all these years, the platitudes we speak about freedom and obligation had finally taken on a real meaning for me. I had fought and risked my life for the freedom to speak my mind, and now I felt I had a humanitarian obligation to do so.

I continued to receive letters from my sisters, and I also wrote back. We were able to exchange news about how they were, and especially about how our children were growing up. Moon-hee often expressed a desire to meet all of my family—Young-ja and my sons, Richard and Alexander—before she died. At the time, she was only sixty years old (seven years older than me), but when I visited in 1983, she looked like she was already eighty. This was certainly due to hard labor outdoors in all kinds of weather and to poor nutrition. I also think it was caused in part by emotional suppression. At least, that was my interpretation based on my thirty years as a practicing physician.

One item that appeared in every letter from my sisters was a plea for money. I had left a large sum for them during my trip, and I knew that they had been able to spend it in the special foreign-currency stores for products not available on the open market.

At first I sent $100 at a time. My feeling was that most North Koreans earn about $25 per month, so $100 was a huge stipend by their standards. As time went by, however, the requests got larger and larger–eventually making their way well into the thousands of dollars at a time. It took me awhile to figure out that my sisters probably weren't getting most of the money I was sending. The North Korean government was desperate for foreign currency that could be exchanged for medicines, hard goods, and, as we eventually learned, nuclear technology.

I desperately wanted to help my sisters and their families live better lives, but I would not become a pawn in a political game. Eventually, with great reluctance, I cut back drastically on the amount of money I sent and simply hoped that all or part of it benefited my family. The entire game made my heart sick.

Chapter 3

When I had visited my mother's grave in Myongchun in 1983, the husband of my second sister, Ok-bong, reminded me that it was Korean custom to move a grave seven years after the body had been interred. He asked in behalf of my sisters that I consider returning to Myongchun to take part in moving Mother's remains to Chu-ul in fulfillment of her final wishes. He mentioned that the family was depending upon me because, by tradition, I was now the owner of the grave. I also received letter after letter from Moon-hee in which she begged me to bring my wife and sons to see her before she died.

I felt a deep obligation to move Mother's grave to Chu-ul, where our ancestors were all buried, and I wanted to show my American family to my sisters, but I faced a dilemma. I hoped to make the second trip with Young-ja and my sons, but Young-ja was extremely fearful about what might happen to us if we all ventured to North Korea. She had a good reason to refuse to go to North Korea with me, for such a trip might adversely affect her family in South Korea. However, by late 1985, because of my continuous insistence, my family agreed to accompany me.

In the spring of 1986, once again with the help of Mr. Chun in Toronto, I received an official letter from the North Korean government, stating that I could take my entire family to North Korea to visit my sisters. I purchased round-trip airline tickets to Beijing for the four of us and made hotel reservations at a Holiday Inn in Beijing. We were supposed to leave on June 16, as soon as our children's summer vacation started. However, late one evening a week before our anticipated departure, Young-ja told me with extreme agitation, "Honey, you go alone. I am really afraid of going there with you. I cannot go. Please excuse me, dear." Her face was a little flushed and tightened, and her voice was moderately harsh and high pitched.

Then my younger son, Alexander, instantly added, "I'm also afraid to go, Dad. We might not be coming back home from there." Then, with a more relaxed expression and a calm voice, he said, "Dad, last night I had a bad dream about the trip. In it, all four of us were detained in a dark, small cell in North Korea by those Communists, like we were prisoners. I tried so hard to climb up that high wall to escape, but each time I tried to reach the top of the wall my hands slipped and I fell down to the floor. When I got up this morning, my hands and entire body were soaked with night sweat, and I was exhausted." He concluded with little tears in his eyes, "Dad, I want to stay here with Mom."

After a short silence, my older son, Richard, then twenty years old, spoke out with a calm voice. "Dad, where you go, I will follow." Then he gave me a gentle tap on my shoulder. This blunt, mature gesture made me content. But the fact of the matter (according to what Young-ja later told me) was that Richard was as fearful as his mother and brother. However, I had made him feel that it was his duty as an elder son to accompany his father to such a "dangerous" place.

♦

As scheduled, Richard and I landed at Beijing International Airport on Sunday, June 16, 1986. A taxi took us to the Holiday Inn without difficulty. On the way, I was struck by how much everything had changed in only three years. Everywhere I looked, I could see billboards and other signs, advertising Japanese and American products–Sony, Kodak, IBM, and other familiar names and logos. During my brief absence, the city's main commercial districts had been transformed and were now simply bursting forth in what appeared to be a bustling Western-style economy. I noticed, too, that the radio in the taxi was playing nice, relaxing classical music. Three years earlier, I had been bombarded at every turn by strident, annoying revolutionary tunes of no musical merit whatsoever.

The large brand-new hotel was beautiful, totally Western-style, and better looking than any Holiday Inn we had ever seen in America. As we walked inside, it seemed very comfortable, and it was air-conditioned throughout–a real rarity in China. Beneath a huge chandelier hanging over the middle of the lobby, a young Chinese woman wearing an ordinary one-piece outfit and very little or no makeup on her face was playing Chopin classics on a piano. The whole scene seemed otherworldly; it was completely unexpected.

As we stood and listened to the Chopin tunes for a while, I noticed that Richard's face was much more relaxed than when we had first landed, and he was clearly enjoying listening to music he had studied in private lessons for most of his life. As I watched my son's face, I felt relief that he was able to take in this relaxed and familiar scene. All around us were many well-dressed, well-mannered, good-looking young attendants. And there were also numerous Western travelers.

We were met in the lobby by Professor Lin of the Beijing Medical College. He had been my host in 1983, when I had given a cardiology lecture at his school while on my way to North Korea. I was struck then by how much the Chinese were trying to modernize their medical-delivery system. They were hungry for knowledge and completely open to Western ideas and resources. This was in stark contrast to North Korea's system, which was backward and inward-looking. I had been able to tell the Chinese many things they accepted without question, but I had found only closed minds in North Korea, where they had even boasted about their old, broken-down system of medical delivery. I had hosted Professor Lin at my home in 1984, during a six-month educational visit I had arranged for him in the Los Angeles area. I was constantly struck by his hunger for knowledge, his willingness to learn, and his appreciation of being taken under my wing. When I made a similar offer to host a North Korean cardiologist, I was simply snubbed.

Dr. Lin brought me up-to-date as we had coffee at the Holiday Inn. Since his visit to Los Angeles, many Chinese physicians had traveled for extended periods to the United States and other Western countries to study modern medical technology, which they shared with their colleagues upon returning to China. I was assured that the practice of medicine in China's big cities had advanced as rapidly and as thoroughly in only three years as had the outward signs of the Western-style market economy I had seen on my way in from the airport. And still he asked questions, even during our Holiday Inn reunion; there was still so much he wanted to know.

After Professor Lin left, Richard and I checked in—the clerk spoke fluent English—and stopped by our room. Then we had a light dinner at the coffee shop in the lobby. The food was very much like what it would have been in Long Beach. After dinner we strolled around different sections of the hotel. There was a large indoor swimming pool, exercise room, and massage service. I asked Richard to take a swim, and I walked over to inquire about a massage. The middle-aged man on duty had on a white lab coat. I asked him if I could have a massage, and he led me into a small room and instructed me to lay down on a small, hard table. He massaged me reasonably well for a half hour. He spoke very little English, but he showed me his diploma. I was shocked to see that he was a graduate of a medical college. I paid eight dollars to this man, a professional colleague, for his services. It amazed me that a qualified medical doctor was working as a masseur.

Late that evening, we began to hear the sounds of loud music. Following our ears, we came to a large hall in which we could see many well-dressed Chinese people drinking, smoking, and shaking their bodies to modern music. This was nothing like the staid, often prudish behavior I had seen everywhere in Beijing during my first visit; clearly, the People's Republic of China had changed quite a lot in only a few years.

The following morning, Richard and I went to the Beijing embassy of the Democratic People's Republic of Korea for our visas. It didn't take long when I showed the visa officer the letter from his government. He told me he was expecting us.

After obtaining our visas, we hired a taxi for all-day service so Richard could tour the Chinese capital. First we went to the Great Wall. We found a few Western-style hotels near the wall, and many Western travelers on tour–far more than I had seen there in 1983. We even met several South Koreans! After the Great Wall visit, the taxi toured the main streets of Beijing. This vehicle was also comfortably air-conditioned, and relaxing, peaceful radio music was on. There were many more modern, high-rise commercial buildings in Beijing than there had been in 1983, and the streets were well paved with more traffic lanes. We saw thousands of people riding bicycles, and many hundreds of street-side billboards, advertising American and Japanese food and other products.

Most of all, I noticed that the people's appearance and deportment seemed to have improved vastly in three years. I asked myself, deep inside my mind, if the people in my former homeland would have changed, too. If not, I hoped then–and hope still–that they mutate soon, as had the Chinese, before their way of life leads them to irreversible destruction.

Chapter 4

I landed for the second time at Pyongyang's quiet, surprisingly small Sun-An Airport at 4:30 P.M. on June 17, 1986. This time I had no fear or anxiety, and I was well guarded by my faithful eldest son, Richard. He was twenty years old, taller and heavier than me, fit and muscular with wide shoulders from working out regularly in the local gym. What comfort his being there was to me!

When we reached the ground, a chubby little government guide recognized me and came to greet us. He introduced himself as Mr. Cho; he was not the man who had escorted me during the previous trip, but he might as well have been, he was so utterly nondescript. We were also welcomed by two somewhat startled-looking and uncomprehending schoolgirls, who presented us with a bundle of flowers and posed with us for pictures. (I wonder who on earth they thought we were.) Then we were escorted by the new guide to a waiting black Mercedes 220 and driven to our Pyongyang hotel on a smoothly paved freeway, which was nearly deserted of traffic. A portrait of an ageless Premier Kim Il-sung was on the side of every building and at every intersection. As far as I could see, unlike Beijing, there had been no changes during my three-year absence.

After dinner we were given free time, but we had to remain in the hotel, so we wandered around every corner of the small building. There was a place for foreign-currency exchange, a fax machine, and stations for sending mail and telegrams. The merchandise sold at the hotel gift shop was on the order of whiskey with ginseng, wine extract, dried roots, and teas. The majority of books for sale at the tiny book stall were written by or about General Kim Il-sung and his son, Commander Kim Jong-il.

We returned to our room, took a shower in a clean, Western-style bathroom, and slept well and comfortably. So far, I had not seen any signs of anxiety on my son's face, which made me feel good.

The following morning, Mr. Cho, our guide, came to the room and told us that we had about one hour before breakfast would be served, so we were free to take a short walk around the city near the hotel—by ourselves. In fact, he *encouraged* me to take a walk in the neighborhood. It was the first time in North Korea that I was allowed out alone.

Richard and I strolled about a half mile and saw many factory workers and students on their way to work and school. It was shortly after 7 A.M. Along the way, I noticed several ladies who had light makeup on their faces—powder, rouge, and lipstick. They were all wearing one-piece or two-piece outfits with belts, and medium high-heeled shoes.

When we arrived near a pond, we found several small children standing at the water's edge with fishing poles in their hands. I approached them and said, "Good morning, boys. Did you catch any fish?" I am sure I spoke clear Korean, in my northern provincial dialect, but they looked curiously at our faces and said nothing. I knew then that we definitely looked like foreigners to them. North Korean citizens are not supposed to converse with foreigners, so they didn't. I thought: What obedient, programmed children! The next stop was a fish market, where we saw only a few pieces of dried fish; there was no fresh fish at all. Then we returned to the hotel.

After a nice, hearty breakfast, we were scheduled to have a city tour for Richard. We found our black Mercedes 220 awaiting us at the hotel's front door, and we were driven directly to the Tower of the Juche, the cultural-political center of the city. Next we toured the Arch of Triumph, a stone paen to Kim-Il-sung's military prowess, located at the foot of Moran Hill.

The last stop that morning was the Changgwang-won Health Complex, across Chollima Street from the Arch of Triumph. I had visited there in 1983. When we reached the indoor Olympic-sized swimming pool, with its two-thousand-plus-seat viewing stands, we saw boys and girls of the national swimming team practicing. At the suggestion of Mr. Cho, Richard swam a few laps, then did a high dive from the diving board. No one else seemed to watch him, but I was so proud of him. I also felt a sense of appreciation to his mother, who had spent so many hours and days taking him for swimming classes when he was a young boy.

After lunch we went to the Pyongyang Metro, the modern subway syttem that had been completed in 1978 to a total route of thirty-two kilometers served by fifteen stations. We rode to a few stations and then returned to the hotel. That evening we were treated to a "revolutionary" opera entitled *Song of Paradise.*

After dinner we were once again given free time in the hotel. As on our first night, we wandered around in the lobby. This time we discovered a stand-up bar at a far corner, where a young lady was serving alcoholic beverages. There was Johnnie Walker Black, Johnnie Walker Red, and some other kind of whiskey with an English label. There were four high chairs by the booth. We don't drink, so we passed by and continued to the other corner at the far end of the hotel lobby.

There was a sign that said "Discotheque" in English—like the one we saw at the Holiday Inn in Beijing a few nights earlier. The front door was open, so we walked in. The room was approximately eight hundred square feet, with a small wooden dance floor in the center, surrounded by a couple dozen chairs and a few small tables. There were bottles of various liquors, all lined up at a small serving bar. There was only dim light, and American music was playing on a beat-up old tape recorder. I didn't know the tune, but Richard instantly told me, "Dad! It's 'Saturday Night Fever,' by the Bee Gees. It's old-fashioned now, but it was popular when I was in fifth or sixth grade."

There were two attendants, a young woman and a man. The man was the bartender and the lady was the hostess. She was posted at the entrance. We didn't see a single customer. I told the hostess that I would like to dance. "Do you have any dancers available for me?"

"We don't," she replied.

"How come you have no customers?"

"People always come very late," she explained.

As we walked out of the place, I checked my wristwatch. It was almost 11 P.M. I wondered how late is "late" in Pyongyang, where workers go to work at 7 A.M.

We strolled back to the corner bar, where this time we found two Westerners standing and drinking American whiskey. They were talking to each other and looking at the two beautiful hostesses. We approached them, and Richard said, "Good evening. Are you American? My name is Richard, and this is my father, Donald. We're from the United States." It turned out that one of the men was an electronics technician from West Germany, and the other had come from Switzerland to make cartoons, using cheap North Korean labor.

When we told the men that we could not find a single customer in the discotheque and had been told that people come in "later"—even though it was already 11 P.M.—they told us that they had been staying at this hotel for more than six months but had only rarely seen any customers there. The place had been set up, as had the bar, just in case foreign travelers staying at the hotel wanted to dispense with any of their Western currency.

We had to travel in the morning, so we spoke to the men for only a short time and then went off to bed.

Chapter 5

We left Pyongyang with Mr. Cho for Moon-hee's home on the ten o'clock evening train on June 19. Mr. Cho insisted upon carrying our bags along with his own as he led us to the rear coach of the train, a spacious and exquisitely clean sleeping car. Each of the compartments was designed for four passengers. Mr. Cho told me that we would have the compartment to ourselves and that he had been booked into a similar compartment next door. He then set out bottled beer and soft drinks he had brought from our hotel and left us to ourselves.

The train ran all night toward the east coast. At Hungnam the train veered almost due north, following the eastern coastline. We entered the outskirts of Songjin at around 8 A.M. The town had been pretty well destroyed during the Korean War thirty-six years earlier, and now there was nothing on its site but some ruined buildings. It looked like a ghost town, but I explained to Richard that I will never forget this town. It was here that I and many hundreds of other refugees were evacuated to South Korea by a United States Navy heavy transport on the morning of December 9, 1950.

As soon as I said this, Richard got a frightened expression on his face and said, "Dad, if you had not been evacuated on that day by the Americans, you would have remained in North Korea, and your life in these thirty-six years would have been no different from the ones your three sisters have led." After nodding his head a few times and turning his face toward me, he continued in an even more serious mood. "That means you would not have come to America, we would not have been born, and we would not be living in a free nation, enjoying the marvelous lives we live today."

I agreed and told him further that tens of thousands of North Korean refugees and the entire South Korean nation had been saved from the Communist aggression by selfless Allied forces led by the United Nations supreme commander, General Douglas MacArthur. Many people had sacrificed their lives in the forgotten war between June 25, 1950, and July 27, 1953, especially Americans, of whom 54,246 were killed, 103,284 were wounded, 8,177 were missing in action, and 7,000 had been prisoners of war. Of the latter, more than 3,500 had died in prisoner-of-war camps. I told my son that we should never forget it and that it had not all been in vain.

It was sad to think that many people living in South Korea seemed to have forgotten that a war of national survival had been fought only thirty-six years earlier. (Later, when the Korean-language edition of my book *The Three Day Promise* was being printed in Seoul, the publisher persuaded me to change the cover picture from one of me wearing a helmet and army uniform. He believed that such a cover would minimize sales of the book, because the younger South Korean generation doesn't want to talk or read about the Korean War. Though it saddened me deeply, I followed his advice in order for the book to be published.)

At around ten o'clock in the morning, we arrived at Chu-ul, where my family had lived before my escape to the south. There we found a black Volvo awaiting us. We climbed into the rear seat after Mr. Cho climbed in beside the driver, and a county official packed our luggage into a smaller, second car and climbed into it for the one-hour drive south to the cutoff to Bong-gang. From there we turned west for a half hour along unpaved dirt roads, up a slope, at minimum speed. On top of the plateau was a small community of six hundred people, living in a few hundred straw-thatched farmhouses. It was a government-owned pear farm. One of the houses belonged to my eldest sister, Moon-hee.

When our Volvo pulled up in front of Moon-hee's house, we found many members of my family lined up and waiting for our arrival. Moon-hee and her husband had one married daughter with two children, and an unmarried younger son. My middle sister, Ok-bong, was there with her husband and two children, and so was my youngest sister, Jung-hee, who was with her husband, two sons, and two daughters. Also, my second uncle's son and his son were there with two of my maternal cousins. I introduced Richard to each of them. I was quite emotional when I realized that this was the first time any member of my American family had met any members of my North Korean family.

There was an official welcoming party that evening at the small community meetinghouse. There were many people there: my three sisters and their husbands, three of my cousins, Mr. Cho, the community manager, the chairman of the county People's Committee, and the vice chairman of the county Workers' Party. The table was set with scores of dishes filled with a vast variety of food. Each official made a brief welcoming speech, and then I got up and delivered my sincere thanks for their kind goodwill gestures.

The officials and I didn't have much in common to talk about, and I was anxious for the party to end. Mr. Cho must have realized that I was becoming impatient with the small talk, so he made the welcome suggestion that the party should be ended due to the extreme fatigue of the guests, who had endured a nonstop daily agenda and who had a busy schedule the next day. Thankfully, every official in the room agreed.

I was extremely relieved to get away from that group of people. Besides, it really was very late. However, after the children and women went to bed, I remained up with my three brothers-in-law for the rest of the night.

Unlike my 1983 visit, it was during this late-night session with my sisters' husbands that we seemed to comprehend that, as family, we could openly share our inner thoughts. I asked bluntly of Moon-hee's husband, "Brother-in-law, what did you do during the Korean War?"

He replied proudly and without hesitation, "Dong-kyu, I was the commanding officer of an infantry battalion."

"Brother, is that so." And with a little smile, "Where abouts did you fight, mostly?"

"In and around the Inje war area."

I told them that I had been assigned to the reconnaissance company of the 23d Infantry Regiment of the South Korean army, and that I had risen to the rank of sergeant first class while serving in exactly the same location as my eldest sister's husband. We were on different sides of the same front, facing one another as enemies. And I added, "I was once shot in the left shoulder by an enemy bullet in the spring of '51—near Inje. You almost killed me! It could've been a bullet from your gun!" I laughed; we all laughed.

I then turned to Richard, who spoke no Korean, and explained to him that his uncle and I had fought this kind of a war between us, not due to our own hatred, but because we were forced to do so by mad politicians on both sides.

The next subject focused on one of my lifelong puzzles. It was about my father's fate. I told them that the last time I had seen Father was at Kilchu, during our retreat to the south in December 1950. "I was stunned to see Father sitting in front of a house, soaking his sore feet in a basin of water. With him was his brother, my third uncle. Father looked totally wasted. Besides the blisters on his feet, his lips were a mass of fever blisters. His meticulous dress from our days in

Harbin was replaced by ragged clothing. I said to him then, 'Father, good-bye. Soon we shall meet again in the south,' and I rushed off to rejoin the Volunteer Korea Youth Group to which I had been consigned." I had not been able to find Father on the American transport I took to the south, nor by any available means after I reached South Korea and went into the army.

I asked my second brother-in-law, Ok-bong's husband, if he had any clue about what could have happened to Father. This brother-in-law had been an officer of the North Korea Security Police at the time, and he was sent to Songjin with many other police shortly after my transport left on December 9, 1950. He said that there were thousands of refugees from farther away who could not be carried out by this ship and had been left behind. I blurted out, "Did you kill all of them?" But he said they were all made to go back to their own hometowns.

I knew that Father had moved to Pyongyang shortly after our return to Chu-ul from Manchuria in 1945. When Ok-bong's husband visited my father there during an official trip, he found out that my handsome father was living with yet another in a line of young women and that they had two baby daughters. This was the first I knew of it; Richard and I had just learned for the very first time that I have two half-sisters, both more than forty years old, living somewhere in North Korea.

After we compared notes on Father for a while longer, the husband of my youngest sister, Jung-hee, added that shortly after the war ended in July 1953, Mother, who was then fifty-one years old, packed a small trunk and took Jung-hee to Pyongyang. It was Jung-hee's opinion that Mother expected to find Father in the capital. Also, Mother maintained a feeling that he had never left the north. For more than a year, whenever time allowed, in all kinds of weather, Mother combed the streets of the ruined capital, hoping to catch a glimpse of her husband. But her valiant search had been in vain, and for the remainder of her life, she had no further knowledge of him whatsoever.

So, after all was said and done, the end of my father's story remained a mystery to us. We just knew that I had been the last of all of us to see him alive.

Chapter 6

The following morning–Saturday, June 21, 1986–was a beautiful day with a cloudless blue sky, pleasant temperatures in the mid-sixties, and very little wind. When I got up, I found all three of my sisters at work, cleaning and slicing fresh mackerel, cuttlefish, and meat for breakfast. They appeared to be extremely happy.

I saw a small mini-refrigerator in the kitchen area. It had a trademark "National" written in English, and I guessed it had been made in Japan. It had not been there the night before. Moon-hee was taking some meat from this refrigerator, so I said, "It is nice to have a refrigerator to keep fish and meat fresh." Moon-hee then told me it was not theirs, that the county official had arranged to rent it temporarily from another village for my visit. A short time later, Moon-hee's twenty-five-year-old son ran in and said in an excited voice, "Mom, the people down the street are receiving a truckful of new electrical appliances and furniture from their relatives in Japan!"

While the ladies were preparing breakfast, I took a walk with Richard and eleven nephews and nieces to a narrow dirt road that ran between huge stands of pear trees. Richard walked with Jung-hee's two daughters, Kwang-ok, who was then twelve, and Kwang-soon, who was nine. Jung-hee herself had been Kwang-soon's age when I left home in 1950. I remembered well how at that time she enfolded me in her small arms and hugged me tightly to her body. "Please don't leave us, Dong-kyu," she had wailed. "Hide in a hole in the mountainside, and I will bring you meals every day. Please, please, Brother! Don't go! You're the only brother I have." It was so long ago: 4:45 in the afternoon of December 2, 1950. I have never forgotten that moment.

As we walked, I saw antennae on top of one out of every five or six houses. Moon-hee's son explained that North Koreans had access to black-and-white television sets, but that there was only one channel available, put out by a government transmitter in Pyongyang. Television was becoming the best and fastest way for citizens to learn and see what their government decided to do for them. There were more TV sets arriving all the time.

Despite Richard's parentage, he spoke very little Korean. But it was obvious to me as we walked that he and his cousins, who spoke no English, were having a wonderful time communicating, even though it was almost entirely by means of body language. They were singing together from the heart.

As we walked, I felt more strongly than ever how important it is for people to touch one another without the filter of politics and the machinations of governments. I thought to myself how wonderful it would be if only my medical-healing art included the ability to heal the whole world's political ills.

Breakfast consisted of steamed rice, grilled fish, barbecued beef, and soybean soup, which were served with our ever-present Korean kimchee, a fermented, red-hot cabbage salad. Moon-hee sat next to Richard as he finished eating all of the huge bowl of rice she had served him. Later I asked him how he could eat so much rice, especially when I knew he had never before eaten rice for breakfast. Richard replied, "I ate all of it because it was cooked with the deep love of my aunts. I wanted to please your sisters." I was extremely proud of his mature, generous gesture.

After the breakfast table was cleared, Moon-hee brought out four cans of fruit for dessert. She said that she had walked for more than two hours one-way to a foreign-currency store in Chu-ul to purchase the fruit with some of the money I sent prior to our arrival. The cans each had a Russian label. We opened a can of pears, and I gave a few pieces to Richard before putting one piece into my own mouth. I saw right away that Richard was turning his face to the back wall and spitting the pear out on a napkin. I knew why when I took a bite of the piece in my mouth. I had to spit it out, too. It was hard, like unripened pear. I tried a piece of apple from another can, and it was just as bad. The fruit was inedible. I told Moon-hee we could not eat because our stomachs were absolutely full, so she gave the open cans to several of Richard's cousins, who were still in the room. They emptied the fruit cans instantly, eating with great gusto.

I asked Moon-hee why they didn't have any fresh pears, because the trees I had seen in the orchard were full of ripe fruit. Moon-hee explained that nearly everyone living in her community worked in the pear orchard from dawn to sunset, five days a week all four seasons of the year, in every kind of weather. On Saturday everyone attended classes run by the Workers' Party, the People's Committee of the County, or some other government agency. Sundays were free. Every single piece of produce farmed from the community orchard was sent to a government-owned packing plant, where it was canned solely for export. Even if the orchard workers could manage to hide a few pears, there was no way to keep them fresh for any period of time; they pretty much had to be eaten on the spot. The nieces and nephews had eaten the terrible pears and apples with such vigor because they had rarely or even never eaten fresh fruit from the orchards in which their own parents and countrymen toiled. To me, right then, this so-called workers' paradise seemed to be little more than a vast slave-labor camp masquerading as a nation.

I had to go to the toilet, so I asked Moon-hee where it was. She proudly pointed to me, "Dong-kyu, over there. Your brother-in-law made a comfortable new toilet just for you last week." The facility was about fifty feet away, a ten-by-three-by-three room, freshly made from unfinished wood panels. There was a small wood box with a hole cut to fit our buttocks, just like a portable toilet we use in the United States. Underneath was a pit, four or five feet deep. When I got to the new toilet, there was only the smell of a fresh, undried palm tree.

I deeply appreciated what Moon-hee's husband had done for me, and I was impressed with his creativity, workmanship, and, most of all, his sincere consideration. This outhouse was in every way superior to the one the family used, or the ones I had used when I was living in North Korea many years before. Then, our toilet had been only a deep hole with two boards placed parallel for our feet. We squatted over the space between the boards.

The entire family–about a dozen Chung relatives in all–gathered at midmorning and set out in two county-owned Volvos and a truck for Mother's new grave in Chu-ul. Also along were Mr. Cho and five or six town and county officials. We drove out to the eastern coastal highway by way of an ill-kept county road system and turned northward. The coastal highway was the same road on which I had fled south to Songjin as part of the mass of refugees thirty-six winters before. As we drove, I could see that many of the bridges and steep grades were the same ones I had trudged over during that dark week. The roadway was still unpaved.

More than an hour and only ten miles from Moon-hee's house, the Volvo nosed into Chu-ul. From there we drove about three miles to the west. This road brought back many other memories, which I explained to Richard as we drove. For example, after alighting from the refugee train that brought us to Chu-ul from Harbin in September 1945, Mother, Moon-hee, Ok-bong, Jung-hee, and I passed here on the way to see Mother's mother in Taehyang, southwest of Chu-ul. At that time, Mother pointed out the mountainside cemetery, where her ancestors were buried. Now, forty-one years later, we were all about to visit her new grave there. Originally, Mother had been in Myongchun, where she died in 1979 at Ok-bong's house. At the time, the family could not move the body to Chu-ul because of a severe rainy season. Mother's remains were relocated to Chu-ul in 1985 in fulfillment of her final wishes.

We got out of the car on the street side and walked to the summit of the hill through fields of ripening corn. The mountain was not high, but from its peak we could look eastward, out over the blue ocean. Moon-hee showed us our great-grandparents' graves on top of the hill, then the graves of our grandparents. A little lower down, she pointed out Mother's new grave. Her name, Kim Ki-bok, was inscribed on a new stone in Korean hangul characters, and to the right were the dates, "July 5, 1904 —September 19, 1979." Inscribed to the left was, "Owner of Grave: Chung Dong-kyu."

My sisters spread a straw sheet over the ground in front of the grave and arranged various foods, including rice cakes, roast chicken, apples, pears, and cookies. My sisters, my brothers-in-law, and I kneeled and bowed to Mother. I cried out, "Oh, Mother, all your offspring are getting together today. Oh, how I wish I could have seen your face just one last time before you left us." After this brief ceremony, we ate all the food. While eating, I thanked my sisters and their husbands for the effort they had made to relocate our mother's grave to this wonderful spot.

After eating, I presented a proposal I had been thinking about for a long time. "How about making a grave for Father on Mother's left side," I asked my sisters. "Nowhere in North or South Korea have we been able to find any trace of him for these many years. I believe that Father perished on the trek from Chu-ul, on the road to Songjin." Immediately, Moon-hee responded in an angry voice, "Dong-kyu! Don't ever, ever mention Father. How can you forget already that Mother and all of us suffered so much because of his defection from our lives during those long years we lived in Harbin and Chu-ul?" I could not repeat the proposal in the face of my eldest sister's profound anger, but in my heart I knew that I was still Chung Bong-chun's only son. I didn't know if he deserved such a harsh appraisal from my sister, but I accepted then and there that my proposal to make a grave for him next to our mother's had failed.

We drove back to Chu-ul, and then turned northwest to the On-po hot springs. When I was a young boy, one of the joys of living in Chu-ul had been this famous and popular spa, which was visited by people from throughout Korea whose afflictions might be remedied in the warm, sulfurous water. It had been owned and operated by a White Russian man, who kept the property clean before the end of World War II, and it had still been well manicured for all the time I had lived in the area. It was fortunate for me that we had the hot springs nearby, for I picked up a case of scabies on my head during our train journey from Harbin in 1945, but the sulfurous water had cleared up the parasitic skin condition and provided me with an excuse to visit the wondrously beautiful area several times a week for several weeks. I recall that my first walk through this area soon after our move to Chu-ul from Harbin took my breath away, for the fall season had brought the leaves to spectacular shades of yellow-gold and rust red. I had never before seen anything to match this awesome tunnel of living color set against a sparkling blue sky. It was then that I felt truly at home in Chu-ul after spending my entire life in Manchuria. Memories of these springs had always represented home in my thoughts of Chu-ul during my decades-long exile from my family.

Contrary to these warm feelings evinced by the hot springs, there was also a horrible, bitter memory of the place that I could and will not erase. During the war, shortly after the South Korean 18th Infantry Regiment freed Chu-ul from the Communist army, we found several dozen bodies, all female, laying naked and frozen in a roadside ditch past the center of the main grouping of buildings in the spa area. All of the dead women appeared to have been between thirty and forty years old, and each had her hands bound with telephone wire to a wooden pole behind her back. At the time, I was the only medical practitioner in the area, and I had been called upon to examine the corpses. The cause of death was particularly brutal. After shooting the women, the executioners had stabbed each of them repeatedly with sharp sticks. Then the dead bodies had been tossed into the ditch. I was readily able to identify my aunt, the wife of my third uncle. We soon learned why these women had been slaughtered. Without trial or proof of the allegations, all had been executed on charges of aiding the hungry war resisters who had been hiding (as had I) in the hills around Chu-ul before the arrival of the South Korean troops.

I did not know then and I do not know today what good was supposed to flow from those brutal executions. But, as I looked on the scene once again in 1986, I knew that the entire Korean nation, northerners and southerners alike, had within my own living memory succumbed to the insanity of a fratricidal civil war. And I had seen the worst of it here, beside these beautiful healing waters.

I was quite shocked, following my long absence from these well-remembered springs, to note that the beautiful scenery and most of the facilities had a seedy, unkempt air about them. But I nevertheless savored taking a bath in the springs, especially because Richard and I had been unable to bathe or shower since leaving Pyongyang three days earlier.

After the bath, we all walked a few hundred steps down to view the suspension bridge over a particularly beautiful stretch of river gorge. I was overcome with nostalgia, for I had crossed the bridge with a young girl named Chun Hae-jean during my first puppy-love romance in 1948. Lost in my reverie, I could almost hear her laughter in my ears when I expressed my initial willingness to venture out upon the insubstantial and swinging span.

So, all in all, the tour to the hot springs brought back good and bad memories of the years long past. And, of course, the same can be said for trip to see Mother's new grave. It gave me an opportunity to dwell on my many loving memories of her, but of course they were bittersweet memories, too, for I knew that she was gone from me forever. And the bitter business with my sisters over our father had been no salve, either. But it was a good day, nevertheless, for it cleared some blots from my soul. And, as I would come to realize in days ahead, it helped me focus upon a suitable contribution I could make in the future.

Chapter 7

The day following my visit to Chu-ul–Sunday, June 22, 1986–was clear and cloudless. At Richard's request, we were to visit a school. We arrived in Bong-gang Junior High School around 11 A.M. and, to our surprise, in spite of very short notice from the night before, there were at least a hundred schoolchildren from kindergarten age to senior high-school students, plus school officials and several teachers, dressed in their best clothes and lined up on the school ground to give us a warm welcome.

First we were invited to the school auditorium for a special music program in our honor. The program, which was presented by the music and art clubs of five local schools, was an hour long and, I must say, very touching. The band played, and the children sang and danced. I was particularly delighted to see two of my nieces, Kwang-ok and Kwang-soon, participating. It was a superb performance, and Richard and I were very proud that members of our family were involved. After the music program, we all trooped outside to the playground and watched gymnastics displays accompanied by accordion music.

When it was time to leave, we found all the students lined up by the school gate to see us off. They clustered around us, each and every one of them, reaching to clutch or merely brush our hands. We heard their little voices say over and over with genuine enthusiasm, "Oh, Chung, please come back. Come see us again!" I wish it was so easy!

Following the school tour, we all went for an outing to the lakeshore just behind the pear orchard community. A few young men from the community had come to the lake early in the morning with scuba-diving suits and had brought up a few hundred clams. There was a cook assigned to this outing from a community restaurant. When we arrived, she was preparing a huge iron kettle of clam chowder with potatoes and rice, seasoned with chopped green onion, sesame powder, and sesame-seed oil. We all took turns stirring the chowder.

As I spoke with the adults, I saw that Richard was playing in the shallow end of the lake with all of his newly met cousins, girls and boys. What a happy feeling and peaceful scene it was.

We all enjoyed the food tremendously, and afterward all the adults sang together the popular songs of the past—"Yang-San-do," "Nodool-gang-byon," and "Arirang." I am still touched by that singing, even after hearing and seeing us so many times over the years on my video. Whenever I view the videotape, I always wonder why Koreans from all around the world can't get along like that all the time.

After dark that night, we started a Chung family—only party. Mr. Cho and other officials were not invited. Twenty-two relatives attended. The youngest was Kwang-soon, Jung-hee's nine-year-old daughter, and the oldest was Moon-hee's mother-in-law, who was an eighty-two-year-old grandmother. There was only one 60-watt light bulb hanging in the center of the ceiling, and there was no fancy musical accompaniment, not even a background tape or record player music. There were only people; so, with warm hearts and loving thoughts, we simply started to sing. My sisters started off, and then their husbands joined them for a song. Then I was added to the three couples, and we sang "Wol-mi-do," one of the most popular new patriotic songs of the day in North Korea. The children also sang, and Richard followed them with humming. For a finale, when all the adults sang "Yang-San-do," Moon-hee's mother-in-law got up and danced. Her hair was totally gray, but her spine was still very straight, and her performance brought back yet another memory to me.

In December 1947, some thirty-nine years earlier, I fell in love with one of the freshman girls who danced the *sung-mu*, the Buddhist monk's dance, during a special music program at the medical-technical high school in Chongjin. She was Chun Hae-jean. At the start, she stood at the center of the stage, motionless as a statue, but as soon as the twelve-string Korean lute sounded, she began her dance. First her fingers, then her hands, then her shoulders, waist, and finally her legs moved in a smooth rhythmical flow. At the end of the dance, I was roused from my reverie by the cheering student audience, rising as one in a standing ovation. Still mesmerized by her performance, becoming once again a part of the crowd, I realized she had all unknowingly stolen my heart. I was fourteen years old.

This happiest of all Chung family celebrations lasted well into the middle of the night–and without any political organization's interference. As I viewed and experienced this lovely measure of freedom in that small *on-dol* room that night, I wondered if such a feeling of kinship could be expanded to encompass the entire Korean nation, north, south, and to the far shores to which Koreans had made their way in the long decades since our schism. At that moment, I believed it could, and I still pray that it can.

Dr. Chung visits his mother's grave in Chu-ul.

*When Dr. Chung walked on the suspension bridge
at the Chu-ul hot springs, he thought of his first puppy love,
with whom he had crossed the same bridge
for the first time in 1948.*

Drawings by Myong-su Shin

Students of the Bong-gang High School present a special musical program for their honored guests from America, Dr. Chung and Richard.

The Chung clan's outing at the lake.

Moon-hee's mother-in-law performs a traditional dance at the clan's private party.

Dr. Chung's nieces, Kwang-ok and Kwang-soon, beg their long-lost uncle to return again soon to Bong-gang.

*The train carries Dr. Chung and Richard to Hyesan
for the trip to Mount Paektu.*

*Dr. Chung and Richard pose at Cheon-ji Lake,
atop Mount Paektu.*

Chapter 8

On Monday, June 23, 1986, we stayed at Moon-hee's most of the morning and early afternoon and talked about living in Harbin and life in America. We also took videotape pictures and photographs. Mr. Cho returned in the middle of the afternoon to tell us that we had to be on our way; Richard and I were scheduled to tour another part of North Korea, and so this was the end of our family visit. The time had flown. Richard and I had been in Bong-gang for only three days and four nights.

Moon-hee, Ok-bong, and Jung-hee escorted us to the waiting Volvo and clung to my hands in the moments before we had to get in. As the car started to move with increasing speed, we saw through the rear window that Kwang-soon and Kwang-ok were waving and crying out, "Uncle, Richard, don't leave us! Please! Please! Can't you stay longer? Can't you come back to stay with us?" They were running, but the distance between them and the car grew and grew until we could no longer see them.

We drove back to Chu-ul, where we took a train to begin the long journey to the Paektu-san, a mountain of considerable importance to all Koreans. From there the train ran along the east coast, passing through many tunnels toward the area south to Kilchu. Then it turned northwest to Hyesan.

On the following morning, we got off the train and transferred to the same Mercedes we had been assigned in Pyongyang. Somehow it was waiting for us there. From Hyesan, we drove very slowly northward on country roads along the Korean side of the Yalu River. The journey took the entire day.

In the evening, we checked into the Samjiyeon Hotel and dined with Mr. Cho. After dinner we ran into two Westerners in the lobby. They were both biologists from Eastern Europe, who were in North Korea to collect certain insects for their research.

The next morning, June 25, the hotel receptionist told us, "You are very lucky because the snow on the road to the Paektu-san has finally melted, so the car can go up." He told us that many people had come from America and Japan a few days earlier but could not visit the mountain because of the snow.

We left for the Paektu peak around 10 A.M. As we were driving up to the higher altitude, the air was fresh, and trees and plants were scarce and stunted. When we reached the peak, considerable snow on the narrow mountain road still had not melted. Our driver attempted to push through this spot, but he was unsuccessful. However, an army jeep arrived behind us within minutes, and six North Korean People's Army officers got out and moved the snow off the road with their small army shovels and gloved hands. Then they let   us go ahead. As we were passing them, I said, "Thank you, officers." I am sure that they did not know I had been a South Korean army sergeant during the war. Ironically, this day was the thirty-sixth anniversary of the start of the Korean War.

Within about 150 yards of the peak, we had to get out of the car and walk the rest of the way. At first there was very heavy fog, and we could not see even a few steps ahead. But the fog cleared off as we reached the summit.

At the peak, a young woman guide in uniform with a handheld portable speaker explained to the visitors the significance of the peak and of Cheon-ji, the lake at the top of the mountain. "Our Great Leader, General Kim Il-sung, fought against Japanese invaders to liberate our fatherland on or around this peak." And then she went on at great length to explain Kim's triumphs in chronological order.

I am not a historian and did not learn about Korean history because I attended school during the Japanese occupation. But I had been told that the mountain is famous not only because it is the highest mountain in Korea, but also because our history and race started from there. In any event, Paektu-san rises nine thousand feet, right on the border between North Korea and China. We could also see Cheon-ji Lake. As the guide droned on about her Great Leader, I thought: What a beautiful, God-given place this is.

The 480-mile-long Yalu, North Korea's longest river, flows westward from Cheon-ji Lake, along the border all the way to the Yellow Sea. And the 325-mile-long Tumen River flows eastward from the lake, along the border to the East Sea (Sea of Japan). The water in this lake was tranquil, and we could see vast mountain peaks on the Chinese side reflected on its surface. Richard shouted, "Yi-ho!" toward the Chinese side, and soon the cry echoed back to us. Too soon, heavy fog again blanketed the entire mountain, and we had to hurriedly take the last of our photographs.

It was our special privilege to visit such famous and important places during our trip. I had been given the opportunity to visit Korea's most beautiful eminence, Mount Kumgang, during my 1983 trip. For these experiences, I must sincerely thank the North Korean officials who hosted my tours.

After lunch at the hotel, we drove out of the mountains and spent the night at a government-owned motel in the old hot-springs town. There were four separate duplex guest houses built with logs. Ours was very clean and equipped with a shower, toilet, and color television. Four beautiful ladies served dinner at the guest-house restaurant. The food was cooked vegetables from nearby fields, fish, and meat. The ladies stood around us, serving food throughout the meal. After dinner we took baths in the hot-springs tub and then watched a music program televised from Pyongyang. We both had a good, dreamless night, but as I was falling asleep I could not help but think about Alex and Young-ja, who had refused to accompany us on this wonderful journey.

Before breakfast the following morning, Richard and I took a thirty-minute walk around the area with the four serving ladies. We learned from them that there were more than seventy employees living in this complex and that most of the guests were foreigners, especially Korean nationals living in Japan. However, we were the only guests staying there that day.

The four ladies were in their early twenties; they were all beautiful and wore very light makeup and one-piece outfits that came to the knees. The fabric was pink with white polka dots. We took photos as I asked about the inn. When I asked if they were married, one replied, "We are all still unmarried."

I asked why, and another answered, "We haven't found the right person."

So I said in a jesting tone that they did not seem to comprehend, "What is the right person?"

One of them replied without hesitation and in all seriousness, "First of all, he has to have the same ideology." I asked no further questions.

I sensed that the people had changed somewhat since my trip three years earlier, when the official had not left me alone for a moment to walk or talk with ordinary citizens. Now I felt free to converse with anyone, and they apparently were free to converse with me. It was much more natural, and I felt more at ease. The people I had met so far seemed open and honest. If I did not like everything I heard from them, I at least felt that their answers were from the heart and not staged for my benefit.

In the late morning on the following day, we had to leave the hot-springs inn for Hyesan. When we walked out to our car, we found a dozen employees, including the four serving ladies lined up at the front of the inn. As soon as our Volvo moved, I heard, "Oh, Chung and Richard, please come back soon to see us, please." They were all waving their hands. I kept watching them through the rear window until I could no longer see them.

We drove west and south alongside the Yalu River. We could see villages and farms on the Manchurian side of the river, on our right side, and nice Chinese music was playing on the car radio. The music was quite different from the strident tunes we heard on the North Korean radio; it gave me a feeling of peace and tranquility. In spite of some winding unpaved country roads, the trip seemed to go by quickly because of the relaxing music.

We arrived at Hyesan late in the evening. Having eaten lunch on the road, we proceeded directly to the railroad terminal. Mr. Cho guided us to a sleeping car. The clean, well-furnished car was filled with foreign travelers and only a few North Korean citizens. When Mr. Cho led us into one of the compartments, I saw that it was not as luxurious as our previous train accommodations. Richard took the top bunk and I was on the bottom bed on the same side. Right behind us, a stringy North Korean who appeared to be in his late thirties walked in and collapsed on the top bunk opposite ours. Then a slightly balding man in his late fifties or early sixties took over the bottom bunk. He wore a North Korean official avocado uniform and appeared to have a dignified demeanor, or perhaps he was snobbish.

I was excited and pleased to share the room with these two men. This was only the second time I had had an opportunity to talk with North Korean citizens other than my relatives and the government officials assigned to accompany me. This kind of contact had been virtually nonexistant during my previous trip.

Shortly after we were under way, the train stopped at another station, where many salesladies on the platform were shouting *"Bap saseyo,"* and I saw many civilian travelers from other cars buying the boxed food. It was dinnertime, and Mr. Cho had obtained food for Richard and me from a restaurant in Hyesan. We opened the boxes he had given us and had a wonderful dinner of all kinds of food.

As Richard and I started to eat, the older North Korean in the bottom compartment, with his well-fed face and portly physique, opened the dinner box he had brought in and proceeded to put away a meal of steamed rice, a few pieces of cooked beef, two hard-boiled eggs, a few pieces of dried sea weed, and kimchee. He ate his entire meal without looking up or talking to us or the other man on the top bunk. His cheeks and nose were greasy and his face was flushed from eating so heartily.

As the older man finished eating, the man who was occupying the top bed sat down on the floor between the tiers of bunks. He looked quite different from the older North Korean. I could tell after twenty-six years of medical practice that he was not well. He unwrapped his dinner, which consisted of a few rolls made of rice, eggs, and meat wrapped with seaweed. After eating quite a few of them, he took out his dessert–hard candies nicely wrapped with thin sheets of edible paper and a variety of cookies. He asked aloud if anyone cared to share the dessert. The bald man said no, but I accepted a few pieces of candy. According to the labels, it was made in Japan. As I ate the sweet, the chubby older man, who was noisily picking his teeth, got up from his bed and walked out of the room.

Immediately, the younger man got up from the floor. He stood at the open door and looked at Richard and me while also attentively watching the outside corridor. As he stood there, he told us his story.

Dazzled by Pyongyang's propaganda campaign depicting North Korea as a paradise for Koreans, he was one of more than ninety thousand ethnic Koreans who were repatriated from Japan, mostly in the 1960s. He said that he had emigrated to North Korea about ten years earlier. Apparently, the North Korean government had assured these people that they would be given better job opportunities than were available to them in Japan, if only they would return to their homeland. The man was given a job, but it was deep in the countryside. He told me his exact job, where he lived, and why he was going to Pyongyang, but I dare not mention it for his sake. He also told me that he wanted to go back to Japan and had tried many times, but such attempts were invariably unsuccessful, and one result of his requests was that he was watched very closely. On the other hand, he acknowledged that Koreans living in Japan were not treated fairly, and that such discrimination had been the main reason for his taking up residence in North Korea. He didn't say so, but I gathered from the gist of the conversation that he would have preferred freedom and discrimination in Japan to discrimination and open distrust in North Korea. In fact, he was a foreigner in *both* countries—one in which he had been born and one he thought of as his homeland.

Knowing his situation was not good, one of his uncles living in Japan visited him every few years and gave him much-needed gifts such as electrical appliances, blankets, and dried foods. The uncle also usually gave him a considerable sum of Japanese currency before leaving. The young man said, "I cried so much to follow him at the end of each of his visits. I definitely made a wrong choice years ago to come back here voluntarily. It was my biggest mistake, and I hope no other person has made such a stupid decision. Essentially, nothing resulted from the promises that were made to us."

While still carefully watching the corridor, he continued. "The food the bald man was eating is specially prepared only for high-ranking officials. Most of the ordinary citizens cannot even find such food to look at, much less eat. Oh my! I wish I could buy one of the dinner boxes out there to show you." All of a sudden, his face flushed, and he bolted inside and climbed into his bed. The bald man was coming back. We didn't have another opportunity to converse.

Our train arrived at the Pyongyang Central Railroad Station at 8:30 A.M. After breakfast at the hotel, I had a visit from Dr. Chang Sin-hyuk. He was still the hospital coordinator at the central government's public health department, at which he had given me an exhaustive and exhausting but extremely enlightening briefing about North Korean health-care delivery during my 1983 visit. When he told me he had come back this morning to give me a follow-up briefing, I wondered if he was going to admit that the North Korean health-care system was far behind those of most nations of the world.

After an hour's presentation, Dr. Chang asked, "Dr. Chung, we have recently imported more-sophisticated and advanced medical equipment, and we have begun inviting guest speakers from the outside world to learn from us and share their knowledge. Can you bring some of your colleagues in America to conduct lectures here, especially in such fields as neurosurgery and liver-transplant surgery?" This was a surprising request, coming from Dr. Chang. Three years earlier, he had proclaimed to me that every health-delivery system in his country was superior. I thought to myself that Dr. Chang had become more honest and realistic since my last visit; he was no longer covering up how far North Korea was lagging behind the times.

When the briefing was over, Mr. Cho arrived at my room with Moon-hee and her son. We all had a nice lunch in the hotel restaurant, and then at my request we went to the largest foreign-currency department store in the country. Many such stores have been built in Pyongyang and most of the other major cities. The store we went to was supposedly built by a joint venture with a wealthy Korean national living in Japan. The goods these stores offered were mostly imported from Japan, but some items were from the United States, the Soviet Union, and other nations.

After browsing for an hour, I told Mr. Cho that I wanted to buy a color television set for Moon-hee. He simply nodded, signifying his approval. I picked out a nineteen-inch Sharp made in Japan, for which I paid approximately $365 U.S. dollars. I also found her a good-sized Soviet-made refrigerator. I wanted to buy a refrigerator for each of my sisters, but there was only one in the whole store. I gave sufficient U.S. currency to Mr. Cho and asked him to find two similar refrigerators in other department stores and deliver them to Ok-bong and Jung-hee. He accepted my money and said it would be no problem.

I was happy to know that all my sisters and their families would soon be able to store fresh, unspoiled food. And I especially liked the idea that Moon-hee, who had been my substitute mother when I was a young boy, would be eating fresh food from the new refrigerator while watching nice music programs on her new color television.

My reverie was broken when Mr. Cho finally got around to telling me that, according to new information from the airline ticket office, our return tickets were not available. He said there were too many unexpected foreign dignitaries leaving North Korea that Friday. The alternative option given to us was to wait until the next flight to Beijing, which was the following Tuesday. This was not good, because we would miss our connecting flight to America on the morning of June 30. So, in the end, we decided to take the train to Beijing on Saturday.

Midmorning on Saturday, June 28, the same Mercedes took us through a light summer drizzle to Pyongyang Central Railroad Station to begin the twenty-four-hour journey to Beijing. There I once again said good-bye to my dearest eldest sister, Moon-hee, who cried and cried as she hugged me close and urged me to come back to visit her again as soon as possible.

Compared to our previous train trip, the accommodations were luxurious. In fact, they would have been luxurious anywhere in the world. We had our own stateroom in what I gather was a first-class sleeping car. I'm not sure why they did it, but I imagine that the North Korean government spent a fortune making one last good impression on the Westernized doctor from Chu-ul and his son.

While the train was crossing the long Yalu River bridge connecting North Korea with China, right next to the Yellow Sea, Richard suddenly began expressing his feelings about our journey for the very first time. "Dad, I am so glad that I came with you. I know now where you were and came from, and I learned how the freedom that South Korean people enjoy today was earned when they fought in the war. I really salute you and your generation's sacrifices. I also saw with my own eyes and felt with my own skin and heart how miserable and difficult life without freedom is. Dad, how soon do you think your sisters and my newly found cousins can visit us?"

I replied, "Who knows, Richard, but history is funny. I am hoping that someday in the near future maybe some kind of improved understanding can be exchanged."

"Dad, what can I do to speed things up?"

"Well," I told him, "you could tell more people about what you just witnessed with your own eyes and ears."

PART II
Repaying Freedom

Chapter 9

Once back in the States, following my second home visit, many organizations invited me to share the learning experiences I had had in North Korea, which remains an unknown place to most of the Western world. In the meantime, my memoir manuscript had been continuously rejected by various literary agencies and publishers.

It took on the average six long months from my submitting the manuscript to receiving the rejection letter. The format of the rejection letters was quite similar. Each read something like, "Your manuscript was read by our reviewers. It seems to be well written and informative. In order to make breakeven as a publisher, we have to sell at least ten thousand copies at $17.95. However, we don't see such a prospect for an autobiography written by an unknown person such as yourself. We have to decline your manuscript, I'm afraid, for lack of confidence that it would fare well in its present form. This was a very close decision. We could easily be wrong. We hope you will show the work elsewhere, and we wish you luck with it."

When I informed Joseph C. Goulden, a widely read author of Korean War history who had reviewed my very first manuscript draft, he said, "Don't surrender just yet. The publishers take a commercial view. Sadly, interest is of secondary consequence in the publishing field, which is why our best-seller lists are laden with books about diets, how to care for a cat, and how to achieve sexual bliss through yogurt and jogging. One becomes cynical."

However, such rejections never discouraged this old soldier, who has beaten so many odds in a lifetime. Rather, the experience gave me the opportunity to polish the text. I spent many hours at different public libraries to read up on related subjects.

It was my thought that the best time to market my book would be during the 1988 Seoul Olympics. But the opportunity was not there. The Olympics came and went without the appearance of *The Three Day Promise*.

Finally, I grew tired of the stream of rejection letters and signed a contract to publish two thousand copies of the 406-page book through a vanity press in Florida. I just wanted to share my life story with people with whom I associate or work.

For the next step, I needed some well-known person to write an introduction for my book. I called Joseph Goulden in Washington, D.C. As soon as I inquired, he said, "Chung, do you know that your former commanding general, Eighth United States Army, Korea, James A. Van Fleet, is still alive? He would be the best man to endorse your book." He gave me the general's address and phone number. He also told me that the Korean War Veterans' Memorial Advisory Board, chaired by General Richard Stilwell, was still raising funds to construct a national war memorial in Washington, D.C.

On the following morning, I sent a letter to General Van Fleet in which I summarized the contents of my book and requested that he write an introduction. I thought the chances of his acceptance were very, very slim, for I had only been a private first class in a Republic of Korea infantry reconnaissance company, and he had been the highest-ranked general in Korea during the war. To my delight and amazement, I received a personal call from the general one morning within two weeks of sending my letter to him.

"I received your nice letter," he said. "It would be my great honor to write an introduction to your beautiful book, *The Three Day Promise*."

In a shaky voice, I said, "Thank you, General, sir." I also decided then and there to accept General Van Fleet's gracious invitation to visit him at his home in Polk City, Florida.

Young-ja and I boarded the plane bound for Orlando on Friday, January 29, 1988. The following morning, we left Orlando in a rental car and headed for Polk City, which is about midway between Tampa and Orlando. We followed the general's directions until we reached Van Fleet Road. We turned in and continued driving about two miles on a curving country road. Spying a mailbox on a post by the roadside, we saw the number of the general's address, although there was no name identification. We continued on into the confines of a huge estate. Finally, at the end of a blacktop road, we saw a one-story main building with a small annex on the left, which I later learned contained an indoor swimming pool.

In front of the house on a tall flagpole, the Stars and Stripes fluttered in the gentle morning breeze. There was no well-defined driveway, the lawn was not manicured as one might expect, and dust hung heavy on the surrounding foliage and structures. It seemed as though I had driven into a deserted and neglected domain, and when no one answered my knock on the entrance to the main building, I felt certain of it.

Undeterred, I found my way around the annex and came upon a lady swimming in a large pool. I waved to her, and she shouted directions for getting into the house: "Go to the main entrance and walk right in. Shout to the general in a loud voice, because he has a little difficulty hearing."

On returning to the main entrance, we ran into General Van Fleet, who was coming out to greet me, because he had expected me to be on time. "Hello, Dr. Chung," he called out. It was exactly 10 A.M., the appointed time!

The general appeared to be about six feet tall and well fit. He was wearing a white shirt, black slacks, and a red sport jacket. He carried a walking cane in his right hand.

After we shook hands, he led us into the first room on the right as we entered the house. He called this the "Korea Room." It was decorated with traditional Korean furniture and artwork, given to him by the government of Korea and by Korean friends. He had a large lacquer desk decorated with inlaid mother-of-pearl and a large nameplate with his name in both English and in Korean hangul characters. Behind the desk were two scrolls written by the first president of South Korea, Syngman Rhee, especially for the general. One was to welcome the general's arrival as commander of the U.S. Eighth Army; the other marked the first anniversary of his contribution to the Korean people. There were two photographs of President Rhee on the wall, and a photograph of President Park Chung-hee and General Chung Il-kwon on a corner table.

The general took time to pose with me for photographs behind his impressive desk, after which we moved to comfortable sofas. Then I began showing him galley proofs of my book. I selected certain portions for him to read, one of which began, "On April 15, 1952, Lieutenant General James A. Van Fleet replaced Ridgway, who had replaced General MacArthur when MacArthur was relieved of duty by President Harry Truman on April 1, following an open disagreement between the president and the general over the conduct of the war." I next turned to another section describing the Communist First Spring Offensive on the night of April 22, 1951, when the Chinese mounted massed infantry assaults against the United Nations lines. When I recounted how I had been involved in this battle as a leader of a squad of twelve Republic of Korea (ROK) reconnaissance soldiers, the general became very excited and described how he had conducted this battle.

For more than an hour, this conversation about the Korean War exploded passionately between the commanding general in charge and a mere infantryman. I had to remind him to call me "Private Chung," rather than "Doctor"! We waxed sentimental over our mutual recollections, and I experienced a rare feeling of contentment in conversing with a fellow participant who was as eager as I to share memories of our times under fire.

After an hour, we left the Korea Room and entered the general's study, where we talked about his autobiography, *The Will to Win,* which was scheduled for publication at the end of the year. Next we were served a luncheon prepared by his daughter that consisted of roast chicken, steamed rice, a vegetable, salad, and hot tea. The general carved the chicken, removed the skin, and served the portions with a very steady hand. He admonished me to "please enjoy the rice, even if it's not as tasty as you used to eat in Korea many years ago."

"The rice is delicious," I responded. "This is the kind of food I recommend to all my patients to keep healthy and fit. Even without *my* professional advice, you have kept yourself healthy and young."

General Van Fleet explained that on returning to the United States from Korea in 1953, he began looking for a place to spend his permanent retirement. He chose this two-thousand-acre spread in Florida because he and his brothers spent their boyhood romping in the vicinity and he remembered it with affection. At one time, he told me, he had wild animals and citrus groves on the property, but now his only crop seemed to be sod.

During the luncheon, he turned to me and said, "Are you going to the Seoul Olympics, Dr. Chung?"

I replied that my busy schedule with my patients would preclude such a pleasurable event.

Cheerfully he continued. "Through a reliable source, I have been told that the South Korean government might invite all the U.S. generals who fought there during the Korean War to attend the games."

"Will you go if they invite you?"

"Of course," he quickly responded. "Even with my arthritic knees, I can walk reasonably well with my sturdy cane."

When we had concluded our meal, the general explained that he was obligated to attend a funeral. We both regretted that we could not continued our sojourn into the past. As he excused himself, he urged me to return for a visit at a time when we might spend more happy hours conjuring other days and other times.

While returning from Florida on the plane, I made my firm decision to donate all the proceeds from my book sales to the Korean War Veterans' Memorial Fund. Without the sacrifices of fellow warriors, I was aware, I could not have found freedom and contentment in a wonderful land of opportunity, where privates mixed freely with generals. I was well aware that I had taken advantage of all the opportunities America had afforded me, and I therefore enjoyed my life tremendously, as did my Korean-born wife and our two American-born sons.

As soon as I reached my home, I called General Dick Stilwell and expressed my desire to donate to the fund all the proceeds from my book sales—all two thousand copies, which had a retail value of $15 each. I am sure that the general easily figured out that I could donate up to $30,000 if I sold each and every copy of the book. I also told him that I wanted to contribute toward building a small corner of the memorial, which I knew was really nothing compared to the contributions so many people had made in sacrificing their very lives.

Chapter 10

The shipment of two thousand copies of *The Three Day Promise* arrived at my office in Long Beach just in time for the thirty-ninth anniversary of the start of the Korean War, which would be on June 25, 1989. What a thrill it was for me! I held the first copy of my book in my fingertips and thought, This is the story of my life and a tribute to my mother and to the people who fought for my freedom. I immediately autographed three books and gave one copy to each member of my family—my wife, Young-ja; my eldest son, Richard; and my younger son, Alexander. It was they who had buoyed me up during the years it had taken to attain this wonderful moment.

The first book-signing party was sponsored by the Long Beach Memorial Hospital Heart Institute, and it was held on June 22, 1989. Cocktails and champagne had been arranged, and the background music was provided by three formally dressed members of the Long Beach Symphony Orchestra. The trio consisted of two ladies and one gentleman playing, respectively, the flute, viola, and violin. Fresh flowers filled a four-foot crystal basket that was carved of ice, a work of art designed by the executive chef of the Long Beach Memorial Hospital. Throughout the book signing, as the ice vase melted, droplets refreshed the gorgeous flowers.

Lots of people came. We had prepared food for only 175 guests, but then we had to add constantly with substitutions. The guests formed a long line for autographs. Their presence deeply pleased me. Most of them were physicians, colleagues, nurses, hospital employees, and friends from medical school, church, and golf clubs, as well as a few friends from Palm Desert. I was especially pleased to see Major General Richard Steinbach, who had served as chief of staff to General Van Fleet during the Korean War. His presence added much to the affair.

Between 4 and 6 P.M., I signed more than 250 books, nonstop. Long before it was over, my fingers, wrist, and back were aching severely. But it was worth it. We raised $5,700 at the book signing.

For all that, there was only one news reporter present, Mr. Cho Yun-sung, from the *Korea Times* in Los Angeles. He interviewed me in depth at the end of the evening, and the resulting article took up the entire front page of the June 24 edition, which commemorated the thirty-ninth anniversary of the war. It was the first exposure of my story in Korean society in the United States and overseas.

As far as I was concerned, the book signing and even the lone article were a complete triumph and vindication of my heartfelt efforts. Together they gave me hope and set me on a course toward wider exposure and broader horizons.

Despite the publicity it afforded, the front-page interview in the *Korea Times* failed to boost book sales. I did not feel I had enough resources for a campaign of paid advertisements, but I continued to self-market the book by whatever means came to hand. Initially, my primary target was of my own patients, who came to see me because they liked me. Most of them did not refuse an opportunity to purchase an autographed copy. It was rather shameless of me to sell books in this manner, but I told them that it was my life story and that all of the $15 they paid for the book was to be donated to the Korean War Veterans' Memorial Fund. Most of them said it was a fair deal and bought the book.

The next marketing target was composed of employees at the hospital. We had more than four thousand people on the payroll, but I did not have too much success with this group. Every time I went to the hospital to make rounds, I carried four books in a tote bag made by a patient that had "Korean War Memorial Fund" stitched on the side. I asked everyone I encountered, "Would you like to have my autographed book? It is my life story, a Korean War memoir, for fifteen dollars, which I will donate to the Korean War Veterans' Memorial Fund." Many of them bought, but not most of them. I marketed the book the same way every Sunday at my church, but there were few sales there as well.

I even carried the books every Wednesday to my golf club. After playing for four hours with three or four other members, I routinely went into the clubhouse. This extended social hour was the most opportune time for my marketing efforts. After exchanging small talk, I told whomever I was with, "By the way, I wrote a book about my life story." Every one of them naturally asked me what the book was about, and I told them I was from North Korea, had fought for South Korea, and had come to America in 1962. I added that my American dream had come true, "And so here I am today." Seven out of ten club members I spoke with bought one or more copies of the book, and I don't think most of them were motivated by the donation. I think that well-off, successful people like to read success stories. Needless to say, I played with different members at each round of golf.

Chapter II

In spite of my aggressive, energetic, and sneaky marketing tactics, I was able to sell only a few hundred books in a month of hard labor. By then, I realized that I would not be able to find many more potential buyers using the tactics I was currently employing, and the number of books I was selling in a given week was rapidly diminishing.

At the breakfast table one morning in late July 1989, Young-ja, who knew my book sales were moving nowhere and that I was exhausted, gave me an idea to send an autographed book to "Dear Abby" along with a letter stating my intention to donate the entire proceeds to the Korean War Veterans' Memorial Fund. This was precisely the common-sense logic that attracted me into proposing marriage to Young-ja in 1965, following a romance by letters between St. Louis and South Korea. I had to admit to her, however, that I didn't know who this Abby person was, so she showed me one of Abby's columns she had saved and told me that Abby had written columns in the past that supported raising funds for the Korean War Veterans' Memorial.

The following day, I fired off a letter and a copy of the book to Abigail Van Buren, and I immediately began an impatient vigil for a response. After about six weeks, while playing golf on a Wednesday with yet another potential buyer of my book, I was paged by my office. I immediately answered the call with my cellular phone. My receptionist told me that I had just received a call from someone at the office of "Dear Abby." I asked if I had to return the call right away, but the receptionist had been instructed by the caller to allow me to finish my golf game; I was to return the call in the morning.

I can hardly express how excited I was about the call. Furthermore, surprisingly, the number turned out to be in the Los Angeles area. I had had no idea where Abby's office was until then. I had mailed my book to an agency some-where else, a long way away. Naturally, I could not concen-trate on the golf game, and I wished only to complete it as soon as possible. I was certain that the call meant that Abby had decided to go along with my request. That was strictly my own way of interpreting the situation, but I *wanted* to think that way. For the rest of the day, I was a very, very anxious man.

Midmorning the following day, I dialed the phone num-ber I had been given, and one of Abby's staff answered. He said that Abby and all of her staff had read and enjoyed my "wonderful book," and that Abby was willing to help my cam-paign by printing my letter in her column. Then he gave me step-by-step instructions for the readers. He told me that my letter would appear on the same day in about twelve hundred daily newspapers in practically every corner of America and everywhere abroad where the *Stars and Stripes* newspapers were delivered. He said that my story would be seen by as many as ninety-five million readers of the "Dear Abby" col-umn. Furthermore, he anticipated that I would receive three thousand to five thousand responses *daily,* according to their past experience. Then he asked me, "Is it true that you have printed only two thousand books? You must have many more books ready, and a staff to handle the requests."

All of this brought on a rush of mixed feelings. It certainly gave me extreme joy that my story would be read by so many people all over the world. But, on the other hand, it brought me much anxiety over the preparations I needed to make for this massive campaign. I knew that *the* golden opportunity had just been given, and I must ready myself to take full advantage of it. It was true; I had initially printed only two thousand copies to share with all the people around me—but people *around the world?* Well, I have never been a very good businessman, but who on earth could have anticipated the potential sales opportunity that had just been presented to me.

Next the man told me that the Abby staff had to know when I would have enough books on hand and enough workers or volunteers to handle the mail and the shipping. In the end, he said, "Dr. Chung, you will have to let us know within one week."

I had already spent $12,000 to print the first two thousand copies of the book, and I had told General Stilwell that I would donate all the proceeds from the book to the memorial fund—without taking my expenses. Now I had to find out how much money I needed to purchase these additional books.

Naturally, I related all my joy and worry to General Stilwell, who was in Washington, D.C. He was also extremely excited about the opportunity. At that time, $6 million was still needed to construct the memorial. I asked him how many copies he thought I should print. He said, "Let me think. Whatever additional number of books we print, our committee will pay for the cost of printing and shipping and handling from the proceeds we make from this new campaign."

I continued to press him. "Okay, but *how many,* General?" He could not give me the number I needed to have. In the end, I told him, "I won't tell you how many, but I will order a sufficient number of copies. I will take all the responsibility if we cannot sell them all." He agreed to this rather blunt proposal, which was really a sign of my stress. Immediately after this discussion with General Stilwell, I phoned my publisher in Florida and ordered the second printing.

Over the next two days, I recruited the equivalent of two infantry squads of volunteers. Many were retired patients of mine, including CPAs, bank executives, and schoolteachers. I also recruited friends from my Sunday School and from my country club. The recruitment was very easy; I could have signed on many more people if I thought I would need them. I was really touched by the interest everyone showed.

Within a few more days, Young-ja and I were invited by Abigail Van Buren for a lunch meeting at the Polo Lounge at the Beverly Hills Hotel. We met on August 16, 1989. General Stilwell, the chairman of the Korean War Veterans' Memorial Advisory Board, flew in from Washington to attend, and the three of us arrived at the lobby of the hotel fifteen minutes early.

At noon sharp, Abigail Van Buren walked into the lobby. We introduced ourselves all around and then walked out to the garden in back of the main building for a photo session at the request of TV and newspaper reporters from the Korean community media in Los Angeles. Abby even knew where we had to stand for better pictures. The picture of Young-ja, myself, and the general with Abby turned out to be one of the best memorable pictures I have ever taken.

After the photo session, we all went into the restaurant. Abby sat between me and Young-ja and directly across from the general. Right off, she asked, "Dr. Chung, what kind of doctor are you?"

I was feeling a little bold, so I replied, "Abby, I mend broken hearts."

To this she instantly replied, "If that is so, Doctor, then I am your partner." This was said with a beautiful smile.

She also had a sensitive discussion with General Stilwell about the women cadets at West Point. The conversation between them became somewhat heated.

After the lunch and before we left, Abby said, "We get more books than we can count," and then she explained what had led her to call me. "My staff saw that *The Three Day Promise* is about the Korean War. Since I have been a supporter of the memorial, they passed it along to me. I read the first chapter and was hooked. I didn't close that book until the last page. I knew that others should read the book." She also told me that the reason for the long wait to publish my letter was to get it in at the best time for the most advantageous marketing. I realized that she headed a very sophisticated organization and that everything had been very carefully planned in the best interests of the memorial fund drive. Abby knew exactly what she was doing.

I don't know who paid for lunch. Abby insisted that she should pay because the Polo Lounge is her territory. Then the general said, "I must pay because all the Korean War veterans owe you both so much."

I found Abby to be fun, warmhearted, sensible, smart, and beautiful, and filled with unlimited wisdom. It's difficult to explain how very much Young-ja and I enjoyed the moment with her at the Polo Lounge.

Chapter 12

A VIVID STORY OF THE KOREAN WAR

FRIDAY, DECEMBER 1, 1989

DEAR ABBY: Last year you solicited contributions for the Korean War Veterans' Memorial. Your readers responded with a total of more than $350,000. You are to be congratulated.

Abby, the Korean War has a very special meaning to me because I am a Korean man who fought in that war.

I was a young medical student in 1950 when the United Nations forces liberated my small town in North Korea. I quit medical school to join the Korean army. (We North Korean refugees were forced to fight for South Korea on the front lines.) Miraculously, I was one of only 26 survivors from the refugee forces.

When I left my home in North Korea, I promised my mother that I would return in three days. Little did I dream that 33 years would pass before I could return to my homeland.

After the war ended, I found myself on the streets of Seoul, broke, with little hope of fulfilling my dream of returning to North Korea and becoming a doctor.

Then fate intervened when a former professor, whom I accidentally met on the street, offered me a job and the opportunity to apply to a local medical school in Seoul!

If the old saying "Adversity builds character" holds true, I am a prime example, because I not only graduated from medical school magna cum laude, I was offered an internship at Barnes Hospital in St. Louis—half a world away, in the United States of America!

Today, I am a well-established physician and have authored several textbooks on cardiology, which is my specialty. I have a thriving office practice and am enjoying a splendid home life with my wife and our two sons in Long Beach, California.

I salute all American servicemen and women who participated in the Korean War, which gave freedom to hundreds of thousands of refugees like myself. That war was not forgotten—those of us who fought in it will never forget it.

Abby, I know that you have very little time for outside reading, but I am taking the liberty of sending you the book I wrote titled, *The Three Day Promise*. It is the story of my life.

If you think your readers would enjoy it, I will make it available to them for a donation to the Korean War Veterans' Memorial. I will leave it to you to set the price. Every penny that the book brings shall go directly to the Korean War Veterans' Memorial.

                    DONALD K. CHUNG
                    Long Beach, CA

   DEAR DR. CHUNG: You were right. I have very little time for outside reading, but after reading the first chapter of *The Three Day Promise,* I was positively hooked! I didn't close that book until I had read the last page—which is the ultimate compliment for a 400-page book.
   You gave me an intimate view of life in North Korea as seen through the eyes of an eight-year-old son of a poor woman who raised her family in a war-torn country. Yours is one of the most fascinating, educational, and inspirational books I have ever read. What a wonderful Christmas gift it would make for teenagers, and also for adults who enjoy reading for pleasure as well as expanding their knowledge.
   Readers, to obtain Dr. Chung's book, *The Three Day Promise,* send your check or money order in the amount of $15, made out to Korean War Veterans' Memorial Fund, to the following address: Donald K. Chung, M.D., 2865 Atlantic Ave., Suite 253, Long Beach, CA 90806.
   One hundred percent of your money will go to the Korean War Veterans' Memorial, and it's tax-deductible.

                    ♦

   Phone calls started coming in from everywhere, mostly Korean War veterans themselves. And service clubs as well as churches were asking to book me for speaking engagements. I was extremely excited—and busy answering most of the calls in between patient care. Somehow my patients didn't mind the interruptions, but rather they were proud of their doctor's popularity. Some people even asked me, "Are you still continuing to take care of us?"

"Of course," I assured them, "My first priority has always been to take good care of all my devoted patients."

The following day was Saturday, and every office in our professional building was closed, but I knew the mail was delivered around 11 A.M. I couldn't wait, so I went to the office at nine o'clock and sat alone with the curtains opened and the front door unlocked.

I tried to read some medical journals, but my eyes were blurred because of extreme anxiety. Somehow this brought old memories from a time I had been miserable all night after I fell in love with the young girl who had danced during the musical program at the medical-technical school in 1947. I had slight tremors, and my mouth was dry with anticipation. I kept getting out of my chair to fetch drinks of water or to pace the room.

At last eleven o'clock came. The mail carrier did not come yet, so I walked out of my office and went through the main entrance to stand outside the building. As soon as I got outside, the mail carrier got out of her jeep, holding a plastic tray. She smiled and said, "Dr. Chung, we have so many letters—a whole boxful for you today."

After she left the mail tray, I emptied all the letters into a large grocery bag and took them home. Then I emptied them onto the floor of my den and started to count and spot-check the return addresses. There were 565 altogether from nearby Los Angeles County alone. Just overnight!

I started to read a few of the letters. All of these people wrote their letters right after they had read my letter in the "Dear Abby" column the day before. The envelopes didn't contain just book requests and checks, though; many included long, heartfelt letters from people whose lives had been touched by the Korean War.

On the following Monday, I knew I'd probably receive a lot more mail, so I moved all the patient appointments to between 8 A.M. and noon and called the first twelve volunteers of the two volunteer squads I had recruited and asked them to come to my office at noon.

All of the seven women and five men arrived by noon. The mail carrier came a little later than her customary schedule. She stepped out of her Jeep at the side of the building and brought in three plastic mail trays. It took a long time simply to count the number of envelopes–a total of 5,785!

As if I had been a platoon commander, I asked the volunteers first to open the envelopes, then separate the checks and make out the mailing addresses in front on each. Stan Jacobson, one of the retired CPAs in the group, made a deposit slips for all the checks. When we had completed the deposit slips, Stan went to a bank inside Memorial Hospital, where I had already opened a checking account for the Korean War Veterans' Memorial Fund.

We first attempted to process the orders and prepare for mailing the fourteen hundred books remaining from the first printing, which I had stored in my office. It was a big task. Some letters gave unanticipated instructions, such as asking that one book be sent to a sister in Hawaii, a second book to a brother in Alaska, and a third book to himself, and so forth. Many of them also requested my autograph.

Most of us worked until midnight. And some other volunteers brought snacks and soft drinks to the office, which they shared with the rest of us. It was hard work, but there was a warmth and happiness built around the good we knew we were doing.

On Tuesday, the fifth day after the "Dear Abby" column appeared–wow!–almost six thousand more letters were delivered. Our fingers were sore from opening so many envelopes, our wrists were swollen, our eyes became blurry from reading all kinds of handwritten addresses, and our backs were aching from the unfamiliar labor.

We thought that we had been well prepared for this massive campaign, but we were facing so many unexpected difficulties, problem after problem. We were swamped, and we were falling farther and farther behind in processing the orders.

In the late afternoon on the fifth day, Abby herself called me to ask how we were managing all the mail. I am sure she knew what to expect, based on her previous experience. I told her my twelve volunteers were flooded with tons of mail, that we were exhausted already, and could not keep it up.

"Didn't I warn you?" Abby said. "Why don't you buy an automatic letter opener. You can open five thousand to six thousand letters instantly." Wow, what a lady! She had a solution for us. I know how to diagnose and treat a diseased heart, but she can treat all sorts of other human problems.

One of the volunteers, Warren Moore, a patient of mine for many years, was a retired Bank of America local branch manager. He knew what an automatic letter opener was and where to buy a used one. He spent all that afternoon going around to different places and came back late at night with one for which he had paid only thirty-five dollars. The idea from Abby was excellent, and the sum was well spent. Mr. Moore opened more than five thousand envelopes with the opener in less than three minutes. Without it, I and my volunteers would have had to stay at my office all night. Thanks to Abby, again.

After midnight, we cleaned up my office for my morning medical practice. I stepped outside for the first time since 6 A.M. I was hungry, exhausted, somewhat shaky, and aching all over. I started my drive home very slowly and carefully. It was a cloudy night, and the moon was invisible.

Insidiously, moments after I set out, one of my war memories came vividly to mind. The Chinese Communist First Spring Offensive had gotten under way on the night of April 22, 1951, when twelve People's Liberation Army divisions mounted a massive infantry assault against the U.N. lines.

The Chinese divisions cracked General Van Fleet's line at the weakest point, which was held by the ROK 6th Division. We disintegrated.

At the next moment, I found myself in the middle of a curving on-ramp, entering from Atlantic Avenue to the San Diego Freeway south. Apparently, I had hit the railing with my front bumper. The slight impact slowed me down and shook me up. I knew I didn't have any injury when I opened the car door and stepped outside; there was no damage to the car.

I bet God in heaven warned me by this minor accident to save my life. God knew I had to continue my campaign to pay my debt to those who had sacrificed their lives to give me the freedom I am enjoying today. I am sure if the accident had happened on the San Diego Freeway, I could have been killed, and then the campaign would have been in deep trouble without me, the platoon leader.

The rest of the way home, I encouraged myself with the knowledge that I was the ex-infantry reconnaissance company squad leader who had survived massive Chinese assaults; the problems arising from the fund-raising campaign were definitely easy by comparison, and I would therefore solve them.

On Wednesday morning, the sixth day, I knew we could not keep up with handling this mountainous task. We were getting farther and farther behind. We had mailed out all of the original fourteen hundred books.

It was during that first hectic, nearly overwhelming week of the effort that Edward Check, a retired Long Beach fireman who was a patient-volunteer, suffered a heart attack while making one of his numerous trips in his pickup truck with books to the main post office in Lomg Beach. That certainly opened my eyes to the stress that my volunteers were experiencing! Ed nearly died, but in the end he pulled through after a couple of weeks of hospitalization.

Mr. and Mrs. Vernon Mortenson took over Ed's job the same day he went into the hospital. Also, Mr. and Mrs. William Edwards, Mr. and Mrs. Sidney Vining, Mr. and Mrs. Sam Whitehouse, and Mr. and Mrs. Norm Svensrud came every day. These were all retired senior citizens, and I am sure the work was exhausting for them, but they performed the grueling job with happiness to be helping a good cause. Also, Tom Stuart, a local insurance agent, took a couple hundred envelopes to his office every day so his office staff could open them and classify the contents. Edward Organ, an engineer at Rockwell International Corporation, came by every day to go over as many letters as possible and write a brief thank-you note to the people I felt had to receive a personal response.

On the morning of the sixth day, I phoned General Stilwell to report that we had achieved sales so far of $265,725. I also told him about our many difficulties. That same afternoon, he called me back to say that he had made arrangements through the American headquarters in New Jersey of Samsung, one of the giant corporations in Korea, to have the local Los Angeles—area Samsung subsidiary send a computer expert to my office to help my campaign.

Several Samsung employees arrived later that same afternoon, conducted a quick survey, and listed our problems. They told me that they could make mailing labels from the addresses printed on the checks and that they would ship the labels to my publisher in Florida so he could drop-ship the books. I instantly agreed to the proposal and gave them the checks that had been lined up in boxes as they came.

After the mailing labels were printed, William Edwards, a retired postmaster, went to the Samsung office to get the checks back. Then the retired CPA, Stan Jacobson, made out deposit slips, which were endorsed "KWVMF" from a stamp he had had made up. Then Stan deposited the checks at the bank.

On the second day of making mailing labels at Samsung, the computer technician called me to say that there was a new problem. Nearly a hundred of the checks processed so far didn't have addresses printed on them. Unfortunately, these checks had already been separated from the envelopes or letters, so we had no idea in many cases whose they were, mainly because of indecipherable signatures. I never expected this problem; it was the first I learned that an address is not mandatory on a personal check. What a hard way to learn the ways of modern living. Well, unless you encounter, you can't learn.

In the midst of all this confusion, the entire second printing of the book was mailed out, and I had to order a third printing.

During the second week of the effort, mail orders began arriving from abroad—Guam, Japan, Korea, the Philippines, Thailand, Singapore, and most of the Western European nations. I knew that many of these people had read my letter in the "Dear Abby" column when it appeared in the *Stars and Stripes* Pacific and European editions. I had been warned to expect responses from abroad, but I was flabbergasted by their sheer volume.

Chapter 13

As I mentioned previously, many of the envelopes included heartfelt letters from people whose lives had been touched by the Korean War. I saved these letters, which number more than six thousand. They are all shapes and sizes, written in pen and pencil, some legible and others barely so. What they share is a type of catharsis.

"Having this Korean man write about his memorable experiences in a war that killed one million of his brethren is a magical experience for these people," Abby said later. "He is sharing his life with them, and they want to share their lives with him."

One reader who wrote to thank me for my book and to order additional copies for friends was Dr. Carl Dubuy, a retired surgeon living in Sparks, Nevada: "The book is the sort of thing that, if you had any idea about what happened in Korea during the war, it brings tears to your eyes," wrote Dr. Dubuy, who was a military physician assigned to the 1st Mobile Army Surgical Hospital, a MASH unit organized during the war. "For someone who has never written a book before, it is a very touching masterpiece."

♦

The effort of responding to book orders was so hectic and tiring that we didn't have a chance even to start reading these letters until Christmas Day. Then, in the first spare moment I had had to myself in more than three weeks, I sat down on my living-room floor and simply picked one at random. It was from a U.S. Marine who had been wounded at the Inchon landing when he was eighteen years old–like me–and had never once been told thank you for his sacrifice.

Using the name and address on the envelope, I found this man's phone number through directory assistance. It was unplanned; I had not thought about doing this at all, but I dialed his phone number. "Is this Earl Knier, of Bergen, New York, a Korean War veteran Marine who was wounded at Inchon in 1950? This is Dr. Donald Chung from Long Beach, California. I am the author of *The Three Day Promise,* and you wrote me after you read my story in the 'Dear Abby' column. Is that you?" He immediately cried and choked up. I knew instinctively that my nose and face were also covered with tears. Barely, with a choking voice, I said, "Earl, on this Christmas Day, I want to thank you for your sacrifice for my freedom in that war." He was obviously weeping and gasping for air–due, I found out later, to crippling emphysema. I was so choked up that I could not continue with the conversation. We both continued to weep until we simply hung up our phones.

So, my Christmas morning of 1989 started with tears of thanksgiving.

The remembrances of these Korean War veterans and their families continually moved me to tears. I cried often as I read them, and I don't know how I read them all, but I did.

I have sought permission to reprint some of them in this book. Many of the veterans and families agreed to share their thoughts in print. A selection of the letters appears in a separate section at the end of this book. These are the words of Korean War veterans, of survivors of Korean War veterans, of Koreans who fought in the war, of young Koreans who really know very little about the war, and of good people generally, whose interest in the war and in Korea came later. To me, they are all quite touching and deeply inspiring. I sincerely thank their authors for sharing them with me, and with you.

By the end of the second month, a total of twenty thousand books had been requested. Nearly all of the first ten thousand book requests had been put in the mail to me on December 1, 1989, the very day my letter was printed in the "Dear Abby" column in the United States. We know this from the dates on the checks. That is amazing to me.

The requests of more than a thousand books *each* came from five states—California, Texas, Florida, New York, and Pennsylvania. Californians by far led the way with 3,109 copies ordered, or 14 percent of sales for the first two months of the effort.

Thanks to all those who supported my campaign and shared the feeling with me.

Sergeant Chung Dong-kyu with his cousin, Colonel Chung Mong-ho. *1952.*

Young-ja and Donald Chung
on their wedding day.
April 11, 1965.

Dr. Donald Chung is greeted by two of his sisters at Pyongyang Airport following a thirty-three-year separation. *1983.*

Dr. Donald Chung at his mother's grave. *1983.*

The author's sisters seeing him off at Pyongyang Airport. *1983.*

Dr. Chung presents
a copy of his
manuscript for *The
Three Day Promise*
to General James
A. Van Fleet.
January 1988.

The Chung family:
Richard, Donald,
Alexander, and
Young-Ja. *1988.*

The proud author
autographs copies
of *The Three Day
Promise* at his first
book signing. Long
Beach Memorial
Hospital. *June
1989.*

Dr. Chung greets Major General Richard Steinback, U.S. Army (Retired) at the first book signing. *June 1989.* General Steinback served during the Korean War as chief of staff to General James A. Van Fleet.

The first media exposure for *The Three Day Promise*, a story run on the front page of the Korean Edition of the *Los Angeles Times. June 24, 1989.*

The delightful pivotal meeting between the Chungs and Abigail Van Buren, with General Richard Stilwell, at the Beverly Hills Hotel. *August 16, 1989.*

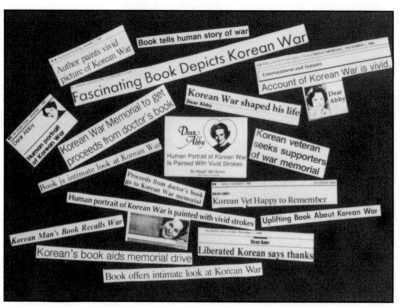

Headlines from various *Dear Abby* columns appearing around the country (and the world) on December 1, 1989.

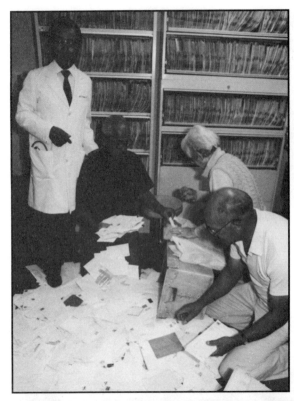

Dr. Chung's squad of volunteers digs into just a portion of one day's mail delivery during the height of the book-selling campaign following the *Dear Abby* column. *December 1989.*

Dr. Chung with only a part of one day's mail delivery. *December 1989.* (By Cristina Salador.)

The Chungs are greeted by President George Bush at the Korean War Veterans' Memorial Fund dinner in Washington, D.C. *May 1, 1990.* General Richard Stilwell also appears.

Dr. Chung with the award presented to him at the Korean War Veterans' Memorial Fund dinner. *May 1, 1990.*

Dr. Chung presents an autographed copy of *The Three Day Promise* to Bob Hope at the Korean War Veterans' Memorial Fund Dinner. *May 1,1990.*

The Chungs are greeted by Rosemary Clooney at the Korean War Veterans' Memorial Fund Dinner. *May 1, 1990.*

Dr. Chung's reunion with his medical-school classmates in Seoul.
May 1990.

Headlines from Korean media stories about *The Three Day Promise*
in Seoul. *May 1990.*

Dr. Chung is made an honorary member of the Korean War Veterans' Association. *July 1990.*

Dr. Chung presents an autographed copy of *The Three Day Promise* to President Ronald Reagan. *July 1990.*

Dr. Chung and Young-ja (far l. and far r.) meet the actors who will be playing them in the Korean television miniseries based on *The Three Day Promise*. This photo was taken, and much of the filming was done, at the Chung home. *March 31,1991.*

The survivors of the 23d Republic of Korea Army Regiment Reconnaissance Company pose with the actors who will portray them in the television miniseries based on *The Three Day Promise*. The company commander, Kim Hyun-min, stands just to the right of Dr. Chung, in the center of the front row. *Seoul, October 1991.*

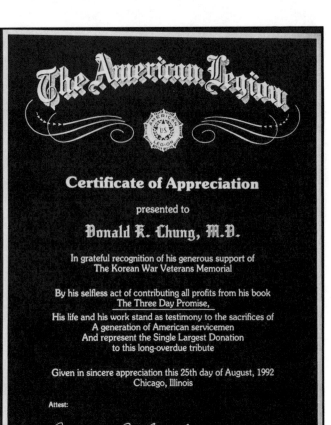

The American Legion

Certificate of Appreciation

presented to

Donald K. Chung, M.D.

In grateful recognition of his generous support of
The Korean War Veterans Memorial

By his selfless act of contributing all profits from his book
The Three Day Promise,

His life and his work stand as testimony to the sacrifices of
A generation of American servicemen
And represent the Single Largest Donation
to this long-overdue tribute

Given in sincere appreciation this 25th day of August, 1992
Chicago, Illinois

Attest:

Robert W. Spanogle
National Adjutant

Dominic D. DiFrancesco
National Commander

Dr. Chung receives an award
of appreciation from Dominic
D. DiFrancesco, national
commander of the American
Legion, during the legion's
annual convention in
Chicago. *August 1992.*

Chapter 14

One day in the spring of 1990, when my book campaign was rapidly tapering off, I received an invitation from General Dick Stilwell, chairman of the Korean War Veterans' Memorial Advisory Board, to be the special guest at a gala dinner.

Dear Dr. Chung,

On May 1, our Board will sponsor a Gala Dinner to honor incumbent Members of the Congress—forty in all—who served in the Korean War. Its collateral purposes will be to increase public awareness of, and garner support for, the national Korean War Veterans' Memorial. The Honorary Dinner Committee will be composed of the top leadership of the Congress; and the President and Mrs. Bush have marked that date on their schedule to attend, the duties of State permitting. Bob Hope will be present in a starring role; the stirring program will be patriotic of motif and long on heritage.

I invite you to be our special guest on this memorable occasion. No single individual–the length and breadth of America–has been as generous of time and resources and accomplished as much on behalf of the Memorial. Having Mrs. Chung and you among us at the dinner will repay, in small part, the enormous debt we owe to a truly dedicated American.

I very much hope that you can accept this invitation.

Cordially,

General R. G. Stilwell, USA Ret.
Chairman
Korean War Veterans' Memorial Advisory Board

♦

On arrival at the Washington, D.C., airport the day before the main event, Young-ja and I were escorted by a Korean War veteran to a black limousine sent by General Stilwell. During the forty-five-minute drive to the Omni Shoreham Hotel, we talked about our Korean War experiences, the war we had fought together when both of us were only eighteen. Like me, he was an infantryman who had arrived in Korea in November 1950 and been assigned to the 23d Infantry Regiment of the 2d Infantry Division.

As we talked, yet another vivid memory of the past rose before me: In the summer of 1952, I had my very first trip to the rear of the combat zone since my arrival in South Korea. I hitched a ride in a U.S. Army three-quarter-ton truck on the edge of a roadway near the front. There was the driver and another man in the front, and two other American soldiers in the rear. At about noon, the truck pulled off the road at the camp of a U.S. Army battalion. The driver motioned an invitation that I join him for a meal. I neither spoke nor understood a word of English then, so I simply tagged along close to my host as we got into the self-service cafeteria-style serving line. Following the driver's lead, I cut myself a thick slab of meatloaf, spooned out steamed mixed vegetables and fresh salad, and took a big bowl of vegetable soup with bread and butter. I was surprised to see that there was still room on my tray, so I grabbed a huge piece of chocolate cake and topped the whole tray off with a cup of hot coffee with lots of cream and sugar. I had not seen so much or such good food since my last dinner with my family before we left Harbin in 1945. Without uttering a single word, I shoveled all this delicious repast into my mouth, using my spoon and fork and, where necessary, my fingers. I ate every last crumb and drank every last drop and even felt a little distress as I pushed my tray away. As we left the mess hall, the mess attendant pressed several chocolate bars into my hand. I could not understand what he said to me, but I suppose it must have been something like, "Hey, Shorty, you look so hungry and you ate so much, you deserve to have these to eat along the way." This was my first real contact with Americans, and I came away impressed and awed with the marvelous meal and the even more marvelous generosity of my hosts. It is something I have never forgotten. Eventually, the truck came to my first stop, Taegu, near midnight. The friendly driver pulled off the main road and drove all the way to the railroad station to drop me off. He offered me his hand, which I shook, and as he pulled away, I bowed over and over again in the correct Korean style.

How had it come to pass, I wondered, that thirty-eight years later I was in a conversation with an American Korean War veteran in English, in a smooth, comfortable limousine in the capital of the world's greatest nation, America.

That evening's dinner was hosted by General and Mrs. Stilwell, and attended by Rosemary Clooney and her escort;

Abigail Van Buren, who was escorted by Dick Adams, president of the Korean War Veterans' Association; and four other special guests.

At last the dinner for the congressmen and President Bush began in the early evening of Monday, May 1, 1990, at the Omni Shoreham Hotel. From the reception desk, we were led to the reception room. There were wonderfully decorated hors d'oeuvres, champagne, and wine, and the music was being played by a dozen or so male musicians wearing old-fashioned Scottish outfits.

Many guests arrived in uniforms bearing medals and decorations. Some were in wheelchairs. I went to most of them to say thank you for their unselfish sacrifice in behalf of the Korean people during the Korean War.

A small group of guests, including Young-ja and me, were escorted by uniformed military officers to a small holding area. We were checked by Secret Service agents at the entrance. After a long wait, we were finally directed to form a line to have a photo session with President Bush, who was the honorary chairman for this dinner.

While waiting some more, Young-ja and I met a middle-aged Korean, who was at the very front of the line. We were assigned a place right behind him. He turned out to be Mr. Kunhee Lee, the chairman of the board of the Samsung Corporation in Korea. Among the others in this group were Mr. and Mrs. Bob Hope and Abigail Van Buren.

Pretty soon George Bush was escorted into the room by several Secret Service agents. The photo session started promptly. After Mr. Lee met the president, Young-ja and I were introduced by General Stilwell to President Bush.

It took less than thirty seconds. Young-ja gave a nice smile, just like the president did, but my expression was that of a man with a severe ache in his body. I don't know how my wife was able to look so natural shaking hands and speaking to the president of the United States. I couldn't even hear her because I was so nervous and excited. I even missed the opportunity to actually shake the president's hand and I couldn't say a word to him. I just stood alongside him with my wife. The cameras flashed a few times, and it was all over.

What do you say when you, an ordinary citizen of the most humble origins, have the opportunity to meet the leader of the free world? What advice do you offer in the advancement of universal liberty and peace? Nothing. None. You say nothing. You smile if you are able, you stare blankly at the camera, and you meekly follow the president's chaperone when your time is up.

Immediately after leaving President Bush's side, we were escorted by another military officer into the grand ballroom. The military band was playing music, and the room was filled with more than five hundred guests, including all of the United States senators and congressmen of the day who had served in the Korean War. We mingled and then we had our dinner.

We were seated with Karl O. Jackson, a special assistant to the president and senior director for Asian Affairs; General David E. Jeremiah, vice chairman of the Joint Chiefs of Staff, and his wife; Mr. Choi Dong-sik, a representative of Hyundai Motors of America, and his daughter; and Major General Donald C. Hilbert, commander of United States Army Military District of Washington, and his wife. They were good dinner companions. General Hilbert had missed the Korean War, but he had served in Korea in the mid-1950s. Hyundai Motors of America, represented by Mr. Choi, had donated $1.2 million to the memorial, the largest single sum from among numerous corporate donations.

As the meal was ending, Bob Hope and Rosemary Clooney performed for the gathering. Then President Bush was introduced, and he gave his speech. He said at one point, "Once this memorial–this fantastic memorial–is constructed, no American will ever forget the test of freedom our brave sons and daughters faced as they sought to stop the Communist aggression."

After the president completed his remarks, the senators and congressmen were introduced. Then Abigail Van Buren. And then I was introduced by General Stilwell: "Dr. Donald K. Chung is a native of North Korea, soldier for the South, American cardiologist with a big heart. For his remarkable creativity and caring spirit, and for his unflagging dedication of self and resources to further our common goal of memorializing those who secured freedom for a nation and its people."

I was presented with the American flag and the flag of California, which were both folded in a glass-topped walnut box made in Korea. The brass plaque inscription reads: "American soldiers on Guard Post Quellette protect a boundary hard won in battle. They flew these flags in honor of Donald K. Chung, MD. Presented with gratitude for unflagging dedication of self and resources to memorialize the heroes who secured freedom for a nation and its people. 1 May 1990."

During these introductions and presentations, there was loud applause from the floor, which made me very excited and then content. I was from a broken family in Korea, from a very small village, but now I stood tall within a few feet of the elected leader of the world's greatest nation and among the most distinguished dignitaries in the capital of history's greatest democracy. I was so proud of myself—and utterly grateful to have been able to fight in that war as a member of the United Nations forces rather than as a soldier on the Communist side. I was also so pleased that life had given me an opportunity to do something significant to help memorialize all those who had secured my freedom.

I hope the memorial will heal a hurt that has lingered in my heart and, I am sure, in the hearts of many Korean War veterans and their families for all these years. Perhaps—just perhaps—if the memorial had been built shortly after the war and all Americans had had an opportunity to reflect upon it, there might not have been a need to build a Vietnam War memorial two decades later.

Chapter 15

During the first week after the "Dear Abby" column, *The Three Day Promise* was rapidly and widely introduced into the Korean community in the United States. In fact, during that first week, KTE (Korean Television Enterprises) in Los Angeles aired a thirty-minute interview with me by reporter Lee Sung-san. And the story was also taken up by Seoul's KBS (Korean Broadcasting Service) special correspondent stationed in Los Angeles, and it aired in South Korea the following day, during the evening news. Radio Korea, in Los Angeles, also aired the interview. And two major daily newspapers, the *New Korea Times* and *Dong-a-Il-Bo* also published the interview story on the front page.

Despite such wide media exposure, however, there were not many book requests from Koreans living in North America. This was extremely disappointing, for it had been my special intention when writing my book to share my story with as many Koreans as possible–to help people of my generation bring back to mind their own experiences, and to let the younger generation know how the freedom they are enjoying today was bought by the mortal sacrifices of many of their parents' generation and the Allied forces.

My desire to introduce the book to the Korean community was so strong that I personally delivered books to every Korean bookstore in the Los Angeles area. I pleaded with the owners to take the books so our own fellow Koreans could benefit from my story. I told each of them that I would donate all the proceeds to the Korean War Veterans' Memorial. I was very convincing; every bookstore I visited graciously accepted the books and agreed to sell them without any margin of profit. I was extremely happy to see them joining me as my campaign was beginning, but book sales were nonetheless very sluggish.

One day in January 1990, I received a very valuable suggestion from a Korean newspaper reporter in Los Angeles. He said, "Dr. Chung, could you please publish your book in a Korean version? Your story touched the hearts of many people of the Korean War generation in the Korean community, because it is not only your experience but also the experience of over ten million members of separated families who are still eagerly and anxiously awaiting the day they can go back to their hometown and meet with the loved ones they left behind forty years ago." The reporter assured me that many of them wanted to read the book but were not buying it because they could not read English well. He also said that my story should be read by the younger Korean generation, whose freedom had been brought about by the sacrifices of millions of their parents' generation and the unselfish sacrifices of the U.S. and U.N. forces.

I had felt all along that I had an obligation to tell my story to every Korean, old and young, but I frankly had not arrived at the simple solution until the reporter suggested it. I set about the task right away.

Translating my original English edition into a Korean one created a whole new set of problems for me. My first language had been Japanese, which I spoke until I was in the seventh grade. This was because most aspects of the Korean culture were ruthlessly suppressed during the

Japanese occupation–including the reading and writing of our distinctive language. Indeed, all Koreans had been forced to adopt Japanese names as part of the program to forcibly assimilate the Korean people. I had also learned a dialect of Chinese in Harbin, but very little Korean–and certainly not *written* Korean. It wasn't until my family returned to its ancestral home in Chu-ul in 1945 that I was able to begin learning the unique Korean hangul alphabet.

Later my years at Chongjin Medical College in North Korea, from 1946 to 1950, had increased my linguistic diet to include Latin, German, and Russian. However, I had no opportunity to truly master the latter three by the time the Korean War engulfed me. I of course spoke and read only Korean when I was a member of the Republic of Korea Army, from 1950 to 1956, and while I was attending medical school in the south. But Korean was very much my second language. In fact, at this point in my life, *all* the languages I have learned to speak and read are second or third languages; I speak and read none like a true native.

I had been living in America for thirty years, speaking and writing English. I could still read and write Korean, but my skills remained rudimentary–too bare for the translation task that lay ahead of me. So I decided to ask a truly bilingual writer to translate the book into Korean.

Finding such a qualified person was not an easy job. After an intense search, I finally found one in Los Angeles, and I asked him to translate only the prologue, for a trial. The six pages of translated prologue were sent back to me quite soon. I read them over many times. The work was rendered in good grammar and beautiful vocabulary, but unfortunately it didn't quite convey the feeling of the original English text.

After examining many other alternatives, I finally called Professor Ko Won, a well-known Korean poet and member of the faculty at the University of California at Riverside. When I told him about my problem, he gave me wonderful advice. He said, "Why don't you translate the prologue on your own, even with your rudimentary Korean language skills. Then send it to me along with the version by the bilingual writer. I'll review both versions."

I knew that my grammar was lousy, and my North Hamkyong Province dialect was quite different from the standard language. And it had been pointed out to me over the years that my penmanship is even worse than that of most other physicians. However, I doggedly followed Dr. Ko Won's advice, and I was able to translate the prologue of *The Three Day Promise* overnight in my own style of broken Korean. I mailed this along with the version translated by the bilingual writer.

When I called Dr. Ko Won a few days later, he said, "I reviewed both sets of the prologue carefully and found that yours has much more feeling." Then he told me that I shouldn't worry about my grammar or writing ability, that an editor at any publishing company in Seoul could easily do a professional touch-up. "You should translate your own story. You are the best qualified to write your own life story."

I am so thankful for his kind suggestion and encouragement. It brought the last part of my dream within reach. A task for which I believed I had no aptitude and no confidence was thus initiated.

Once the job was ignited, I moved swiftly, with my usual aggressiveness and zeal. I needed to use a Korean-English dictionary often, but this was not so new; my nearest companion when I first arrived in America three decades earlier had been an English-Korean dictionary.

Often I became so deeply engrossed in the task of translating that I could not put the job down, and I kept working through the night. When I read the first finished portion, I liked it. I was so pleased with Dr. Ko Won's suggestion and my decision to do my own translation. In the end, I felt the Korean version was at least as good as the English.

The next hurdle was to find a literary agent or publisher in Korea. I was by no means a professional writer or a known author, and I did not know anything about the publishing world in South Korea. As I was pondering this issue, I received a surprise telephone call. It came late in the night in early 1990 from a man in Massachusetts. He said his name was Richard E. Kim. I had never met him, but I instantly recalled that he was the author of *The Martyred,* a highly praised book that had caused a big sensation in the United States and Korea many years earlier. He was also from North Korea and had served in the Republic of Korea Army during the Korean War.

After speaking with Mr. Kim for a bit, I explained my dilemma. He said that he had in fact called to tell me that a reliable publishing firm in Seoul wanted to publish the Korean version of *The Three Day Promise.* I marveled at this incredible coincidence. Once again, as had been happening all through my ragged life, there had appeared yet another valuable helper to ease my task. Naturally, I accepted the offer without a second thought, based solely on Richard E. Kim's reputation.

This good news accelerated my hopes. Now I wanted to have my book released in Korea on June 25, 1990, the fortieth anniversary of the beginning of the Korean War. In fact, the Korean version of *The Three Day Promise* was published in Seoul before the scheduled time, on May 1, 1990. The book was well edited, just as Dr. Ko Won said it would be.

My only regret is that the publisher changed the front jacket design. The marketing people insisted that my picture wearing a helmet and an army uniform should be replaced with a drawing that was not war related. The reason they gave me was that today's younger Korean generation does not want to know there even was a Korean War and will not buy any Korean War—related books. This knowledge made me extremely sad. I only wanted to let the young people know how their fathers' generation had suffered and sacrificed to save South Korea during that war so that they could enjoy the freedom–to sweep us under the rug.

Chapter 16

At 5:15 P.M. on May 11, 1990, Young-ja and I arrived in Seoul to mount a sales campaign to coincide with the release of the Korean version of *The Three Day Promise*. This was my first visit to Seoul since 1979, and only my second visit since I had left there for the United States in 1962.

The publisher had scheduled a very tight itinerary. We stayed at a huge hotel complex called Lotte. Its very large lobby was filled with lots of international travelers, nice live music was played constantly by a piano or an entire live band, and there were many restaurants, serving all kinds of international cuisines. The hotel was also connected to department stores, movie theaters, and grocery stores. It was possible to do and buy anything. This was really a city inside a city.

I was especially happy to be greeted by Young-ja's three sisters, her youngest sister's husband, and their children. This was the second time I had seen them all since Young-ja had come to America as my bride in 1965 following a one-year postal romance. They all looked healthy and happy. I thought then that I wished my own sisters, brothers-in-law, and their children living in North Korea could look as healthy, prosperous, and contented–and that they could make the short journey from the north to Seoul to see us, too, and meet their extended family of fellow Koreans.

The schedule was extremely hectic. I was interviewed by twelve different reporters from every daily newspaper in the country, plus weekly and monthly magazines. I had to repeat pretty much the same story over and over, and soon I was utterly bored with hearing about my own life. Photo sessions for the monthly magazines each consumed two to three hours. Each photographer drove us around to find the "best place" for the background. It was quite an exhausting business.

On Tuesday evening, May 15, a book-signing party was given by my medical-school classmates at a restaurant in the Lotte. The party was graciously sponsored by a lady classmate of mine, Nam Kyung-ae, who like me was a native of North Korea. She had been very supportive of me during our school days, and now was one of the most successful gynecologists in Seoul. I was so happy to see so many familiar faces, fifty-two in all, from a graduating class of 120 men and women.

After the dinner and before the signing of my book to each of them, I was asked to make a brief speech:

"On the morning of April 1, 1957, as I–a North Korean refugee, ex-ROK sergeant first class, wearing a black-dyed army summer fatigue uniform and white rubber shoes–made my way down the hill to the sophomore class homeroom, I was able to see inside through the glass windows that faced the wall. Nearly all the seats were occupied by about a hundred women in their early twenties.

"When I got to the door, I was stopped in my tracks by the pungent odor of your combined preferences in perfume." They all laughed. "I hesitated for an instant, thinking in a flash about how those provocative odors, and all that they implied, would take my mind from the important purpose at hand." They laughed harder. "I had spent nearly six years in an all-male environment, and I had had only an inadequate, celibate seven-month transition at Dr. Park's clinic before taking the giant leap I was about to take. I was not ready for any of the many things that might happen in this predominantly female enclave.

"Most of the students around me managed to fill four or more pages of notes during our first fifty-minute lecture, but I had managed to pick up only a dozen pathology terms by the time the professor slammed his notebook closed and strode briskly from the room. No sooner had he gone, however, than the sweet-looking young lady who was sitting behind me asked if I would care to borrow her notebook to flesh out my own inadequate notes. All I could do was nod my head and stammer my thanks. I needed to do a lot more than just fill in a few blanks, and it was soon clear that she knew I needed more than just a few notes. After the brief pause, she graciously offered to let me keep her notes overnight. I was deeply embarrassed, but I knew I needed any help I could get, and I was so grateful for it. What I really needed, I knew, was an instant grasp of English."

At that point, everyone in the room demanded that I reveal the identity of my benefactress, especially if she was among us that evening. I told them that it was a sweet memory of thirty-three years ago, and it could have been anyone with us. It was a smart thing to say, because Young-ja was in the room, too. There are, I know, limits to this kind of looking back.

I went on to say that I was very happy to see several of my male classmates, who graduated the medical school successfully and passed the National Medical Examination with the aid of my tutorial efforts. It meant a great deal to me to have helped them lead successful, productive lives.

I also reminisced about the moment I received my valedictory award on March 2, 1960–graduation day. It is no exaggeration to say I swear I heard mother's voice whispering in my ear, "Son, you have done a good job. You made me happy. I did not waste my life on you." As these words echoed once again across space and time, I saw Kim Ki-bok's face, with its brown and wrinkled skin, and her gnarled hands, which had never touched me with anything less than total love. Graduation day, for me, had been Mother's day more than my own.

I wanted to appear either by telephone or taped interview on a KBS-TV program. I found a good connection for this project. One of my patients, Mr. Bae Hak-chul, happened to be the president of KTE in Los Angeles. He was a long-serving executive who had been sent to the United States by KBS. He accepted my request and arranged for me to appear on at least one of the talk shows, along with interviews during the news hour. However, due to a labor dispute that erupted just before we arrived in Seoul, nearly all the employees at KBS were out on strike. In spite of the uncertainty of the situation, the president of KTE personally assured me that we would broadcast.

I continued to try to contact the program producer, as instructed by Mr. Bae, starting from my arrival in Seoul on May 11, but I had no success. There seemed to be no sign of a resolution to the strike. I knew I had to leave Seoul on May 20 to resume my medical practice, which is my primary obligation. I was extremely eager to appear on the TV program before my departure.

At last I received a phone call from the producer of the news production. It came early on the morning of Wednesday, May 16, five days after my arrival and only four days before my departure. He told me that he would send a reporter and camera crew to my room at the Lotte at 11 A.M.

What a relief that was! My primary goal was about to be achieved. But as on many other occasions in my lifetime, this had come to pass only after crossing many hurdles and overcoming breathtaking suspenses.

The news crew arrived on time, and the interview was conducted. In the end, a two-minute interview segment was produced for the news show. It covered the essence of my memoirs, the introduction by the "Dear Abby" column, the donation of the entire proceeds of book sales to the Korean War Veterans' Memorial, and my wishes for the quick reunification of Korea. The story was aired on KBS news at midnight and transmitted to all of South Korea throughout the day on Thursday, May 17. The response was immediate and overwhelming.

Most of all, there was a surprising call at 11 A.M. the day of the TV appearances. It was from a man living near Pusan. He was extremely excited. "This is Bang Duk-soo. Don't you remember me?"

I said, "Who?"

Then he continued, "As soon as I saw your face and heard the story on last night's news, I knew that this is the Chung Dong-kyu I know."

I could not remember his name, but his story was just the same as mine. He was one of the northerners from my own province who had been inducted into the 23d Infantry Regiment Reconnaissance Company at the same time as me— one of the few to survive the war. He also told me that he was in contact with most of our other surviving war buddies, including our company commander, Lieutenant Kim Hyun-min. But as we talked, I realized that his accent was typical of Kyongsang Province—South Korean. When I asked about it, he explained that he had married a woman from Kyongsang Province and has been living there all these years.

Bang Duk-soo remembered where we first met. It was in early December 1950, a few days after I had left my home. We met in the schoolyard at Kilchu. There, a number of teenaged boys had joined the Local Volunteer Youth Group in the hope of somehow assisting the retreating ROK Army. I'm still not sure what we thought we were going to do–take up arms, perhaps, and fight the pursuing Chinese army. In any case, the entire body of this group was simply absorbed into the ROK Army immediately upon arrival in South Korea, and we were all assigned directly to 23d Infantry Regiment Reconnaissance Company. Like me, Duk-soo was one of only 26 Local Volunteer Youth Group members to survive the war–of an original contingent of 156.

When I asked him how he remembered so clearly all these things that happened such a long time ago, he replied, "Because my dream to go back to my home and family never ceases for one minute during my waking hours–not in all of these forty years–although I am living happily and comfortably with my wife and our children in this wonderful free society."

Then he asked me in a pleading tone, "Chung Dong-kyu, when can we go back to our hometown? I am already old, as you know. Can it happen during our life?" I could only console him with what he wanted to hear–the hope that the border defenses on both sides would be demolished and that we could indeed "go home" again in our lifetimes.

Among other things, he gave me a phone number for Lieutenant Kim.

As soon as I had a moment–my phone was constantly ringing whenever I wasn't on it, answering the previous call–I dialed the number for Lieutenant Kim, who was also living in the southern part of South Korea. When he answered the phone, I said, "Commander Kim, this is your former soldier Chung Dong-kyu." That was all I was able to say, for I started to cry. I managed to tell him that I had gone to America and was doing well.

In 1950 I was eighteen, and he was only twenty or twenty-one, but he was the commanding officer of 156 new soldiers from North Korea–a god to us. I thought that then–and told him now–that he was a superb leader. I learned that he had stayed in the army and had retired as a colonel after returning from service in the Vietnam War, to which South Korea had contributed one of its elite combat brigades.

For some reason, Kim had made me his unofficial orderly, and he often let me stay in the company headquarters when the rest of the troops went out for front-line offensive assignments. This could well be one of the reasons I survived a period of severe combat. I told him this on the phone, and I also reminded him that in the summer of 1952 he had asked me to deliver the money he saved from his pay to his fiancée, who lived in Pusan. The resulting journey was my first leave in the war, and my very first trip outside the combat zone since my arrival in South Korea two years earlier. It was the first time I had ever met Americans, and it undoubtedly led to my eventual decision to live in America. Also during that fateful journey, I had located my relatives living in South Korea, including my cousin, Chun-duk, who was an officer working at the ROK Army Headquarters in Taegu. And I learned from Chun-duk that my third cousin, Mong-ho, was an ROK Army colonel and the senior intelligence officer on the staff of the ROK 8th Division, at the front. My eventual contact with Mong-ho led to a transfer to his staff, away from the fighting, and to my being assigned as a medical orderly– my first step back to a life in medicine. Thus, in more ways than I probably realize, my close contact with Lieutenant Kim undoubtedly saved my life and put me on the path that led to this time on the phone with him in the vastly changed world of 1990. What an immense full circle it had been!

In my entire hectic nine-day stay in Seoul, this phone conversation with Lieutenant Kim was the pinnacle. For me, it was as good as finding my own father after such a long separation.

Chapter 17

*June 25, 1950: It was just turning to dawn; the outlines of
the mountains and trees were becoming visible. "Storm"–
meaning "Open the attack"–was transmitted to ninety thousand members of the North Korean People's Army, who
had completed their movement to the 38th Parallel on June
23 under the guise of conducting operational training and
planning.*

I still remember hearing the announcement on Radio
Pyongyang that morning: "If the South Korea puppet government does not suspend its military activity near the 38th
Parallel, the government of the Democratic People's Republic of Korea will join the Security Corps of the Department of
Home Affairs to take decisive measures for the smashing of
the enemy. South Korean authorities will be held responsible
for any results of this military venture."

At 9:30 that same morning, General Premier Kim Il-sung
came on the air himself with a "Message to the People of
Korea." Kim said, "The South Korean puppet clique has
rejected all methods for peaceful reunification proposed by

the Democratic People's Republic of Korea and has dared to commit armed aggression against the Haeju District north of the Thirty-eighth Parallel. The Democratic People's Republic of Korea has ordered a counterattack to repel the invading troops. The South Korean puppet clique will be held responsible for whatever results may be brought about by this development."

War was formally declared by North Korea at eleven o'clock that Sunday morning. On the fourth day of the "counterattack," the People's Army seized Seoul.

Task Force Smith–a U.S. Army infantry task force composed of 540 soldiers of the Japan-based 21st Infantry Regiment–was the first U.S. combat force to reach Korea. It took up a position just north of Osan on July 5. Unprepared to face the onrushing People's Army tanks, this American force was obliged to leave all its equipment in the field and retreat.

The entire Korean nation, north and south, had succumbed to true unrestrained insanity of a fratricidal civil war. That war changed my life. The fortieth anniversary of the beginning of that war was also the first anniversary of the release of my memoir, *The Three Day Promise.*

I was asked to do a radio interview by a Korean reporter from the Voice of America, which is headquartered in Washington, D.C. The one-hour interview about the Korean War and my memoir was taped at the studio of the Voice of America's Los Angeles news bureau by long-distance phone with the reporter, who was in Washington, D.C.

When I came out of the studio, I had a brief conversation with the bureau chief, Lee Hall. She asked me about the topic of my interview. When she heard my story, she expressed a personal interest in the subject. She had been a reporter during the Korean War and wanted to tape what we were sharing at that moment in 1990. There was no preparation or rehearsal; we just did it. She later mailed me an edited transcript of the interview, which was to be released as a special feature story. She said, "Dr. Chung, here's the way it came out in English. It will probably be widely translated for use around the world on June 25. Cheers and thanks again." And so it went; I was touching far more people than I ever dreamed was possible.

On the morning of June 25, 1990, I had calls from KCBS-TV and KNBC-TV, both in Los Angeles. They both wanted to interview me. I was very excited; this was my first exposure to American television audiences. But the invitations also caused me extreme anxiety because I had never had any live-interview experience. I told them they could interview me after my morning medical routine.

Reporters and camera crews arrived at my office at noon. Either I talked too much about my memoir and the Korean War Veterans' Memorial campaign, or the reporters liked my story. Whichever it was, the interviews lasted more than ninety minutes—with each reporter. At the end of his interview, David Lopez, from KCBS, handed me $50 from his own pocket, a donation to the Korean War Veterans' Memorial Fund. I gave him three autographed copies of my book.

I was eager to see how this whole ordeal turned out. At last, the first interview aired during the early-evening news hour. It was quite good, and I was thoroughly surprised and gratified. The second interview went just as well. I think it is a testament to good editing that I looked so good and spoke so well on the air.

Another interview, in Korean, was aired both on KTE in Los Angeles and KBS in Seoul. And I appeared live on a one-hour talk show with Tom Snyder, from 7 to 8 P.M., on KABC-AM, in Los Angeles. When I got home that night, I was extremely exhausted, but it was worthwhile. I was accomplishing my mission, telling millions of people that we should not forget there had been a war forty years earlier.

Korean Culture, a Los Angeles—area publication, printed an excerpt of my autobiography in its Summer 1990 issue and commented that it was becoming one of the most widely read books ever written by a Korean American.

On July 23, 1990, I received a plaque naming me an honorary member of the Korean War Veterans' Association. Through this organization, I had the special privilege of visiting with and presenting my memoirs to the former president, Ronald Reagan, at his office in Los Angeles.

After going through security clearance and waiting, I was led into the president's office. After I posed for photos with him, he invited me to sit down on a sofa to talk. While presenting him with a copy of my book, I told him, "This is my memoir, my life story and the Korean War story, sir."

He paused for a moment, and then he said, "I can read this in my free time."

Then I told him, "President, we have a common birthdate, sir. I was born on the exact same date, twenty-one years after you."

He said, "I was in college then."

That was all. My time was up.

Thus, *The Three Day Promise* and my efforts to raise funds for the Korean War Veterans' Memorial were rapidly and widely publicized via American as well as Korean media, including radio and television interviews and newspaper features.

In addition to helping the memorial fund, these combined events appeared to change the South Korean government's view about what they had seen as a pro—North Korea bias in my activities since my first home visit in 1983. In fact, there was a complete turnabout. Far from being threatened or written off, I received a commendation from the South Korean foreign minister, Mr. Lee Sang-ok. Also as a result of my media activities, the South Korea consul in Los Angeles recommended that I be named an advisory board member   of the Peaceful Reunification Committee of South Korea. However, I did not accept the job. My reason then and now is that

I want to remain a devoted physician for my patients without the time-consuming stresses that seem to emanate from politics.

On the other hand, my rising popularity among South Korean politicians and their Korean American political allies seemed to change North Korea's views about my activities. This became evident from phone calls I received from several L.A.-based Korean businessmen following a trip they made to North Korea. According to them, no one they met in North Korea expressed their distaste about my autobiography, but they were nonetheless wondering why I was donating such large sums of money–acquired from book sales–to the "Yankee War Memorial" in the U.S. capital when I should have been sending it to my sisters in North Korea to better their lives. One of the callers even suggested that I donate $30,000 to $50,000 to my sisters, and he further instructed me as to how I could send such a donation in U.S. currency.

Naturally, I could not take such advice because the expenses of the book printing, handling, and shipping were all paid for by General Dick Stilwell's advisory board of the Korean War Veterans' Memorial Fund, which of course ends up with all the book profits. As to the advice to send large sums of cash to my sisters, I had long ago concluded that the cash was disappearing into the North Korean treasury, which is starved for hard Western currency. Besides, I also knew very well that my sisters in North Korea cannot use such large sums of money. (They told me over and over that they are living in paradise.)

One other point impinges on my decision about where I put my resources: So far I have donated $438,000 to the memorial fund to repay America and Americans for my freedom.

So, as my status among South Korean politicians and officials rises, it also sinks in the minds of North Korean officials. To me, all this ideological nonsense is a very sad business.

Let me state it as clearly as I can: I am neither pro—North Korea nor anti—North Korea, nor pro—South Korea, nor anti—South Korea. I remain a proud and grateful American, and I am, as I always have been, a supporter of Korea, my *one* native country.

Chapter 18

On May 30, 1990, I signed a contract presented to me by KBS—TV regarding their intention to produce a Korean-language TV drama based on *The Three Day Promise*.

In August 1990, producer Lee Young-kook and screenwriter Chung Ha-young visited me in Long Beach to plan the production and research locations. They told me then that they were going to shoot fifty episodes of fifty minutes each. I showed Mr. Lee and Mr. Chung my home, the hospital, and my Palm Desert weekend home. I also provided them with information beyond what was described in the book. Throughout their visit, write-ups about the auditioning of actors and information about the production constantly appeared in the Korean-language media in Korea and the United States.

A KBS drama production team arrived in Los Angeles on March 25, 1991, and started filming immediately. This presented a unique experience, and I wanted to be available to assist their work during their stay. I found that the work of cameraman, lighting, makeup, and costumer is as difficult as that of the producers, directors, and actors and actresses.

Sometimes they started work at dawn and continued all night with little or no rest. Almost all of the shooting took place right at my own home, office, hospital, and golf course. It was great fun!

At last, the very first episode aired in South Korea on Monday night, May 20, 1991. The episode began with the true story of my fiftieth birthday, the beginning of my first journey back to North Korea.

It was early morning here when my youngest sister-in-law, Young-sook, phoned us from Seoul. She excitedly described the scene she was watching on her TV screen at that moment. "Brother-in-law, wow! You are driving down the Interstate Freeway 10 to your weekend home in Palm Desert. . . . Wow, sister Young-ja is being shown in your Long Beach home. . . ."

Very soon I received another call from my medical-school classmate, Dr. Nam Kyung-ae, the prosperous gynecologist in Seoul who had sponsored the book-signing party in May 1990. She called to congratulate me and tell me how excited she was to see her classmate's life story on a TV drama.

The first fifty-minute episode was shown on Monday and Tuesday nights in Seoul. Then it was air-mailed to KTE in Los Angeles and shown here on Thursday and Friday nights. This was the pattern as the fifty-part series unfolded. It was also released by KTE to every Korean video shop in all the major Korean communities in the United States. I was told that this TV series was watched by most Koreans in Korea and the United States, especially by North Korean refugees.

Even though this was my own life story, I was absolutely hooked into it. Each week I couldn't wait for the next episode.

Since I opened my cardiology practice in Long Beach in 1972, my patient population has been composed nearly entirely of Caucasians. For years I had not been known in the

Korean community, and I was not even listed in the phone directory in Los Angeles, where almost a half-million Korean immigrants were living. However, I certainly became known to nearly all the Koreans in the Los Angeles area as soon as the first episode of *The Three Day Promise* TV drama aired. It showed me at work in my Long Beach office and at the hospital.

The airing of that first episode ignited another form of chaos, which I frankly had not considered at all. What occurred immediately was something akin to the appearance of my story in the "Dear Abby" column, which led to my being swamped with four to five thousand letters and book orders during the first few days alone.

Beginning the morning after the first episode of the drama appeared on the local Korean station, telephone calls overwhelmed my office switchboard. Either people wanted to share with me right then their own experiences from the Korean War, or they wanted to set up an appointment for a consultation. For the moment, we booked so many consultations that it appeared that a sudden epidemic of heart disease had struck the Korean community in and around Los Angeles. I was soon to discover that, in a way, this was too true.

Understandably, most of the calls were from the Korean War generation, especially North Korean natives, of which there are nearly a quarter million in the Los Angeles area alone. To assist in this new adventure, I immediately hired two bilingual office workers, installed a new phone line for use entirely by Korean callers, and I retained a bilingual phone-answering service in Los Angeles for after-working-hours and weekend coverage.

We were swamped with many new daily appointments, and a few Koreans could be counted upon to show up at the office each day without having made an appointment. Mine is a sole practice with only twelve hundred square feet of office space and eight chairs in the waiting room. We realized that we had to provide more seating for all these new patients, so I had a long wooden bench installed in the corridor outside my office entrance.

The mass confusion began right in the waiting room. While waiting to been seen, the new Korean patients talked excitedly to one other about where they came from and what they were going to share with Dr. Chung. It was nothing like the typical medical waiting room, where people try to cough and sneeze without making a sound. These people were animated and gregarious.

Each morning we took care of our regular patients, but the entire afternoon practice was devoted to the new Korean patients. Most of the Koreans were elderly refugees, living in Los Angeles. They were often brought to my office by their children, or they arrived on their own by taxi or bus. It usually took thirty to sixty minutes for them to get to us by car or taxi, or as much as a few hours to get there by bus. Many of the senior citizens were very frail, and many could barely walk, but all of them were deeply desirous of sharing their experiences of the Korean War with me—enough to endure the ordeal of travel and waiting in my office.

The first new Korean patient was an eighty-eight-year-old woman, born in 1903. As soon as she took her place in front of my consultation table, she grabbed my hand tightly and said, "Dr. Chung, nothing is wrong with my health. I so wanted to meet you. I was born one year before your mother. I never shed so many tears in my life as while reading your memoir. I cried for your mother." This woman's sixty-six-year-old daughter-in-law, who escorted her, told me that her mother had insisted upon seeing me after reading the book, but the family had not been able to find my address until the TV drama began airing. She told me that, while watching the first episode, her mother-in-law had shouted, "Look, that man, the author of *The Three Day Promise* is practicing at Long Beach Memorial Hospital!" And she mentioned that while watching, both of them had cried anew for Kim Ki-bok, my mother.

The older lady continued her tale: She and her husband, with four children, had successfully escaped by boat from Whang-Hae Province, on the west coast of North Korea, to the south a few months before the outbreak of the Korean War. But her oldest daughter, who had already gotten married, could not follow them. If she was alive, she would have been seventy years old at the time of the visit. The patient cried as she said to me, "I beg you to locate her for me." I gave her a tissue and gently touched her hands for a while. I realized then and there that my first flip response to Abby– "I mend broken hearts"–was being put to a critical test. And I prayed that I was an adequate "heart" doctor after all.

The next patient was a sixty-five-year-old lady, who told me, "While passing the Thirty-eighth Parallel in that terrible cold, snowy December 1950, my husband was shot by the Communist army. He died instantly. We couldn't do anything with his body; we had to escape fast. He was twenty-six. Dr. Chung, he was a good man. He hated the Communists. We hoped to enjoy our new lives together in the south. I still miss him." She went on to explain how she had survived through extreme hardships, how she alone had put all three of her children through college. She showed me her hands, which were crippled with severe arthritis. And that brought to me the memory of the last time I had seen my own mother's gnarled hands, forty-one years earlier.

And so it went. The last patient that very moving afternoon was a sixty-nine-year-old woman. Unlike all the others, she was authentically very ill. She had a new artificial heart valve and had undergone extensive surgery for cancer of the pancreas. She was too sick to tell me anything other than her medical needs, but she did manage to say, "Dr. Chung, I too am a refugee from Pyongyang." She gasped for air and went on. "I read your book three times." And then she took my hand in hers and asked, "How is the circulation of your hand now?" She knew from the book that I had suffered from frostbitten hands while serving on the front lines during the war.

Chung's Cardiology Clinic was turned into Chung's Refugee Counseling Clinic.

In addition to my new afternoon patients, I felt obliged to return calls to a number of Korean refugees who lived too far away or were too frail to visit me in person. My office staff selected these from among all the callers. At times, they had to insist that a particular caller not suffer the ordeal of travel from some far-off place. Others I called back because there was not sufficient time to really hear them out during a hectic afternoon at the office. I made the phone calls late each evening and on weekends. The phone work was a new experience for me, but I felt it was necessary if I was to take part in healing emotional wounds that had been affecting their lives for so long.

It finally dawned on me that my work with the Koreans, especially the phone work, was part of a subconscious attempt to relieve some of my own guilt for not having been able to return home before my mother's death. I was in as much need as my new "heart" patients. I had a disease of the heart that I needed to heal by helping others who, like me, had for so long borne the consequences of our common Korean tragedy for all these wasted decades.

Eventually, the pace of the afternoon visits and evening and weekend phone calls slowed to the point where I had a life beyond the office and the phone, but it has continued to this day.

Chapter 19

On Sunday, October 13, 1991, we arrived in Seoul again so Young-ja and I could appear on the "Finale"–the fiftieth and final episode of *The Three Day Promise* TV series. The next day, Monday, I visited with the producer and writer of the 11 P.M. talk show on KBS. On Tuesday I appeared on a one-hour talk show in the KBS studio. There was a live audience, but the show was recorded.

At nine o'clock on Wednesday morning, I met in the KBS studio lounge with twenty-two of my war buddies, all natives of North Korea who had arrived by ship in December 1950 from Songjin and been assigned directly to the 23d Infantry Regiment Reconnaissance Company. They and I were all the known survivors of the 156 original refugee troops. They had traveled from every part of South Korea for this reunion. I was especially thrilled to see our original company commander, Lieutenant Kim Hyun-min.

The youngest member of our company had been seventeen years old in 1950, and the oldest was then twenty-eight. Now we ranged in age from fifty-eight to sixty-nine. We reintroduced ourselves and reminisced about our common experiences of some forty years earlier.

We were together again because Bang Duk-soo, who had called me right after my KBS midnight-news appearance in May 1990, had gone right to work at the time, locating all of the survivors. He had made extensive use of the police networks. In the end, he succeeded in finding every one of them and in organizing the "Three Day Promise Club." Even before my return to Seoul to appear in the TV series, the others had been meeting every three months at a different buddy's town. They had even taken several tours to the former front lines on which we had fought together four decades earlier.

The first place they visited was Jin Ko-Gae, where another soldier and I had been assigned to scout about a thousand yards ahead of our company by moving northward through a line of hills. This had taken place in January 1951 and is described in my memoir. It was where I became an authentic blooded combat veteran.

Late in the morning, we were taken by a KBS bus to Palgak-jung, on the top of Nam-san, in the center of Seoul. We met with the actors who played our roles in the TV drama, and I thanked them for their superb performances in portraying our past in these dramas.

After a photo session and filming by KBS of the drama scenes, I stood with a few other war buddies at the edge of the mountain for a good while, quietly looking out over the city. I saw the famous sixty-three-story building, and many other fine, tall buildings. Below me were tens of thousands of cars, jammed into every street. And millions of people were packed into the vast, sprawling modern city. I was proud to realize that I had once served to protect the freedom of South Korea, and I now knew that our sacrifice—the loss of all those precious lives in the war—had not been in vain. Because of us, half of our countrymen and half of our nation were free.

Late that afternoon, we took a cruise on the Han River, which was kindly arranged by KBS. I made sure I sat beside Lieutenant Kim, who was now actually Colonel Kim. Among other things, he told me that his life was good and that he was happy. He also said he was very happy that a soldier of his had become a successful cardiologist in America and had written a memoir that included the story of our company at war.

Our reunion kept going, and we ended up eating dinner at one of Seoul's best Chinese restaurants, Mambo-Jang. The owner of the restaurant generously sponsored us–there was no bill.

After drinking strong Chinese rice wine and eating ample food, each of us got up to share a few experiences from the war. I heard many thrilling stories I had never heard before, including details of the hardships they, too, had endured in order to survive after the war. All went through things that were much harder to bear than any aspect of my own story. I cried often throughout the evening.

One man made an instant poem and read it, and we sang a few songs together that we had sung often during the war. In the end, they presented me with a commemorative plaque made up with black pearls and reading:

> Dear Comrade, Donald K. Chung, M.D., brought back the memory of the insanity of the fratricidal civil war, the pain of separated families, and the sentiment of family love by writing his memoir, *The Three Day Promise.*
>
> In turn, it gave the opportunity of this reunion of our war buddies of forty years ago through a TV drama series by KBS, based on his memoirs.
>
> Thus we congratulate Dr. Chung's homeland revisit and present this plaque to commemorate this historical reunion of the 23d Infantry Regiment Reconnaissance Company.

The names of the twenty-two surviving refugee soldiers and our three surviving officers are listed at the end.

♦

On Thursday night, the Chongjin Medical College alumni and Professor Park Suk-ryun gave a party in my honor. These were the people I was with from 1946 to 1950. It was always nice to see my mentor, Professor Park. He was well over seventy years old but he still saw more than a hundred patients a day, and he also still presented scientific papers to medical journals and at medical conventions. He was and is really the grand master teacher for me and so many others.

On Saturday, October 19, Young-ja and I appeared with all of the actors for the filming of the final episode of *The Three Day Promise.* And we left Seoul on Sunday. It had been an extremely busy schedule, but it included several of the most memorable moments in my life.

For the airing of the final episode, a party was given at the KTE auditorium in Los Angeles. All of the commercial sponsors of the series through the six-month run were invited. During the week of June 25, 1991, I also appeared on radio talk shows with twelve individual stations from Buffalo, New York, to Alabama to commemorate the forty-first anniversary of the beginning of the Korean War.

Honors and recognition of all sorts have continued to find their way to me. In the past few years, things have quieted down at the office, and my life is back to being my own, though I still occasionally see fellow Koreans who want to discuss their lives with me.

Someday, when I take my grandchildren to tour Washington, D.C., I will show them the magnificent Korean War Veterans' Memorial. And there I will tell them that I not only fought in that great international crusade against Communist aggression, but I contributed to the building of this great monument to the memory of the many heroes who secured freedom for our Korean homeland and our Korean people.

In my lifetime, I want to visit my sisters and their children again. I want to kneel once more beside my mother's grave. But I do not want to take a train or plane from Beijing. I want to drive there from Seoul, past a place I hope we will call "the former Peace Village" at Panmunjom. I want to drive the length and breadth of my homeland—a free and united democratic Korea. If that happens, my life will have meant something, my efforts these past years, since my fiftieth birthday, will have borne fruit. I am a happy man now, but only when my nation is one nation and my people one people will I be fulfilled.

Chung Dong-kyu
Donald K. Chung
1995

PART III
Remembrances
of the
Forgotten War

The following accounts and comments have been gleaned from the thousands of letters I received after the appearance of the "Dear Abby" column in December 1989. These are as many as space permits, but there were countless other poignant accounts and expressions from people all around the world. I thank each of them for writing, and I wish there was a way for me to share all the letters with all the fine people who wrote them.

RUTH BOOK

My husband, Don, served in the army in Korea for nineteen months in the early 1950s. We were married the previous year and working on a farm. Needless to say, since our home and occupation were already established, it was not our choice to cope with a war in Korea. Our oldest son was born while Don was in Korea, and he was thirteen months old before meeting his father. Don and I had many negative feelings about the sacrifice that was demanded of us. After all, neither of us in all probability had ever heard of Korea, so why should we be required to make such a major sacrifice?

Anyway, Don made it home safely and we resumed our life on the farm and raised our family. Our unpleasant memories were put aside but never really accepted or understood. I must admit that I indulged in much self-pity. Now I'm trying to comprehend the degree of suffering the Korean people were forced to endure. Healing comes with time.

This past October [1990], we had the opportunity to return to Korea with Kew Chai. We were gone for only six days, which was not nearly enough time, but it was an incredible trip. Memories resurfaced and were shared. We felt such peace and acceptance of our sacrifice. We take our freedom so much for granted. All these years he just put the past behind us and concentrated on the future and establishing a happy home for our children. There was so much gratification from seeing the results of the "police action." We now have a special fondness for Korea and its people. It is our wish to be able to go back for a longer stay.

DONALD BOOK

The Korean era will always be a part of my life. The saddest thing about the Korean conflict is the little recognition it has received from our government and the American public. With so many casualties, it still isn't considered a war. It's a disgrace that there were so many sacrifices made and peace has still not been achieved after more than forty years. There are few memorials, and this country has never really honored the dead, injured, or missing.

RICHARD C. BRADLEY

The most vivid memory I have of the Korean War is of the thousands of North Koreans forced into small circles on the beach at Hungnam in December 1950. I have always wondered what happened to those people.

You probably came south on the merchant ship *South Wind,* as I did too a few days before Christmas in 1950. There was a new strange smell down in the holds where we slept. It was my first smell of Korean food. On board were soldiers from different units, perhaps fifty different units, who were going to Pusan to set up bivouac areas for troops who would come later.

Everyone was carrying small arms and some had hand grenades. It was probably relief from combat, but many had real bad dreams after we put to sea. Probably a psychologist could explain it: We were safely out to sea and we couldn't hear artillery fire of the battleship and two cruisers accompanying us. But did everyone get into his sleeping bag and have a good night's sleep? No! It was people all night long, jumping to their feet, carbine or automatic in hand, shouting, "Here they come!" No one fired his gun or threw a grenade, but it sure was a bad night.

Korea seems to be an almost forgotten war in the United States. It has become a standing joke among my peers: "Did it really happen?"

APHRODITE PAPPAS BROWN

I wish to remember a classmate from first grade through high school, who was killed upon his arrival in Korea soon after graduating from college. He was Chapman Spencer. Chapman was mentioned in *Pork Chop Hill*, by S. L. A. Marshall, who gives an account of his death in battle. He had the reputation of a very fine young man, and the town of Palmer, Massachusetts, where he was born and raised, mourned him deeply.

FOSTER L. SPENCER

My brother, Chapman T. Spencer, entered the army in 1951, shortly after his graduation from Wesleyan University. He went to Korea in May 1952 as a private first class. He saw action at Old Baldy and Pork Chop Hill, accepting battle rank along the way until he reached sergeant first class at the time he was killed, April 1953 at Pork Chop Hill, about a month before he would have rotated to the States.

Chap was a commendable athlete, and his letters to me indicated that war, to him, was a contest, a contest to win. He was intrepid; he always strove to be the best. He was headstrong with a lot of reasons to be so.

He was killed at Pork Chop Hill in action that is recounted, including the circumstances of his death, in *Pork Chop Hill,* written by the late military historian General S. L. A. Marshall.

Chap's death left an enormous hole in our family (there were no other brothers or sisters), and my parents established a memorial athletic fund in his name at Palmer, Massachusetts, High School, a scholarship I continue to support. In addition, I joined a veterans' group from Palmer during the summer of 1993 in providing a stone in Chap's memory at the Korean War Memorial dedicated by the Commonwealth of Massachusetts.

My mother, Helen Spencer, always felt that my brother was an unlucky fellow. She told me, long before his demise, that Chap was a lot like a cousin, Gilbert Geer, who was killed in action at Saint-Lô, France, shortly after the D day invasion in World War II. So much for a mother's premonitions.

Korea was our generation's war, a war in which American soldiers fought under a flag other than their own, against an unknown enemy. As history, it wasn't much of a war, but for those of us who served, survived, and remember, it remains a watershed–the first sanctioned United Nations military action.

BOB BUTTON

I fought in Korea in 1951—52 with the 23d Infantry Regiment.

In September 1989, my wife, Regina, and I visited Korea through the "Korea Revisit" program sponsored by the Korean War Veterans' Association. It was a fantastic, highly emotional reunion with ROK veterans I am proud to have served with–people who these many years later remain dedicated to maintaining the freedom so many paid such a high price to achieve. We were fortunate to have friends stationed at Uijongbu (I'm a retired army sergeant major); their hospitality allowed us to extend our visit beyond the six-day "Revisit" schedule and see more of the new Korea.

And *new* is certainly the word! I was relieved to read in *The Three Day Promise* that even you, a native of the country, could not identify some of the places you had fought over during the war. I thought my memory was degrading from senility, so alien was the paved and cultivated Korea of today from the Korea I remembered. I was a little sad and a lot proud to see such a vibrant, progressive, industrialized Korea–sad only because my landmarks had been paved over. But that's why we fought, of course, so that life could move ahead and people could go about the business of life. We realize that it's not quite the secure, ideal freedom all of us had envisioned, but certainly it is aeons beyond what might have been, had we not stemmed the tide. It takes no imagination at all to look northward and shiver at what might have been the fate of South Korea.

It mystifies me, though, that a too-large handful of young South Koreans could look upon this contrast and cast their lot with the ideology of their northern neighbors. Can it be, with the Western world finally grasping the ideas of democracy and casting off its dictators, that *any* degree of freedom has less appeal to these people than a totally controlled existence? I'm truly confused by this phenomenon.

DR. CHOE JUN-DO

I often read books, but *The Three Day Promise* touched me deeply and made me shed tears for the first time. The reason is because I had a similar experience in my life.

When I was separated from my parents and family, I promised them I would be back within ten days. But after nearly forty-five years, I have not kept my promise. What an unfaithful son I am to my parents.

When I was leaving my family, my commanding officer told me, "We will be returning within ten days." At that time, my father raised his two hands and said, *"Mansae."* I can still hear him saying *"Mansae,"* which means "ten thousand years," or "long life." Many years have passed, but that moment still comes to me. Now I go to church and send my love to my parents and family in my prayers. This is how I comfort myself.

While fifteen million Koreans who were separated from their loved ones have experienced sadness and tragedies, and waited patiently for the unification of our motherland, Dr. Chung had told the painful experiences of fifteen million people to the entire world.

JAMES M. COSTA

I was born in Fabrizia, Italy, and emigrated to the United States with my parents. In 1947 I dropped out of my junior year in high school, joined the army, and went through jump school.

I was in the 82d Airborne Division when the Korean War broke out, and then I was sent to Korea, where I joined Company A, 23d Infantry Regiment, 2d Infantry Division, as a BAR-man. I was wounded during a long-range patrol behind enemy lines with French paratroopers attached to our regiment.

After my tour with the 23d Infantry, I was sent to the 187th Airborne Regimental Combat Team, once again as a BAR-man. I was severely wounded in action at Outpost Zebra, in the Kumwha Valley, and I lost my left leg as a result of my wounds. I was discharged from the army in 1954, after nine months in the hospital.

Before I left home in 1947, I thought I would eventually finish high school. But I never did. I got married shortly after I left the army, and my parents, who were poor immigrants, needed my help. But I ended up having my own business, a machine shop that makes parts for aircraft.

My four children made up for my lack of schooling: Eric graduated from MIT in the top 10 percent of his class, and he has an M.B.A. from Stanford; Peter graduated Dartmouth with an M.B.A.; Tom graduated from West Point, went to Ranger and jump schools, left active duty as a captain, and now works in industry; and Heidi is a graduate of Notre Dame.

Like so many veterans, the war I went through did not stop me from living. It taught me that life is precious, and so I value simple things, too.

GEORGE R. CULP

Your letter to "Dear Abby" and her reply made me feel proud, as I served in Korea in the U.S. Army, 3d Infantry Division, 15th Infantry Regiment, 4.2-inch Heavy Mortar Company, Communications Section. I was there in 1951—52, And am *very proud* to say I served my country there. It pleases me to see that someone is doing something about a memorial for the Korean War veterans. It seems that the Korean War veterans have been sort of pushed off to the backseat. I think that the Korean War was just as important as any of the other wars and that the veterans of that war deserve recognition.

It hurts to know that you were forced to fight against your own people. I think it is unusual that a North Korean is helping to set up a memorial for the Korean War veterans.

JUNE DeBLOIS

I have always hated the North Koreans because in July 1953 my husband of two weeks was killed on Pork Chop Hill.

Now, thirty-six years later, I still cannot speak of him without crying. I loved him so much.

I realize there are good people everywhere. However, being so young and so naive at the time, I blamed the North Koreans for everything.

I also had a promise once upon a time. He said, "I'll be back in a year." I'm married again now, with four beautiful children, but deep in my heart I yearn for that promise to be fulfilled. I don't think I've ever gotten over the loss.

His name was Robert Earl Lagess. Bob was in Easy Company, 17th Infantry Regiment. He was killed shortly after 6:30 A.M. on July 8, 1953, near Sokkgae, North Korea. It was heavy fighting on Pork Chop Hill. North Koreans were screaming and coming over the hill. There was hand-to-hand fighting, with bayonets, also. Bob was hit in the legs with shrapnel. He was dragged to a ditch or foxhole by men of another company, because Easy Company had been just about depleted. Our men retreated and did not have time to take anyone with them.

I often wonder if he was already dead when the North Koreans got to him, or if he saw his death coming.

He was listed as Missing in Action as of July 8, 1953, and I was notified approximately a week later. We waited approximately six months, and then we had a mock funeral with a flag draped across an imitation coffin. That very morning, when we got home, there was a telegram informing me that his body had been retrieved and sent to Japan for identification with dental records. We had another funeral, with an honor guard and two rows of National Guardsmen from our area lining the way to the church.

I first met Bob when he was our paperboy. I had to pay him one Friday, and we got to talking. I thought he was so cute! And so we started dating. I was seventeen and he was eighteen.

On January 31, 1953, Bob and I were married at Fort Jackson, South Carolina. He had been in the service since

November. We were together four days in South Carolina. Next, he came home on leave at Eastertime, and we were together for ten days. Our married life consisted of two weeks.

Bob was twenty when he was killed; he would have been twenty-one in a week.

Our dream was to be married, have our own little apartment, and a baby someday. I wanted a little boy, like him, and he wanted a little girl, like me.

I remarried in 1955. It was not for love but because I was so mixed up and wanted a baby to call after Bob, to pretend it was his. And so my daughter was born. I named her Roberta Earline, after him. Later on, I had a son, and I named him Bruce, after Bob's young brother, whom we loved so much.

Needless to say, the first few years of my second marriage were not very good. But I had a very understanding husband, who was a Korean War veteran himself. I was told by a professional that I had never come to terms with the death of my first husband, that I was very young and traumatized. I believe this to be true.

How do I feel about the North Koreans now? Well, if you look at the TV, you can see rigid lines of young North Korean robots, as I call them. Has anything really changed? After reading *The Three Day Promise,* I can say, "Yes!" Now, instead of robots, all marching in line, I can look beyond and see the mothers. I can tell by the book that Dr. Chung loved his mother very much, as I loved mine. It is truly a great shame on all of us that our young men go and die for ideals we could settle without force.

Bob didn't know anything about Koreans, north or south. He was told to go and fight, expected to go and fight, and to lay down his life. I now have two sons in the service. As a mother, I can say I do not want them to lay down their lives, not because someone tells them to.

I am sixty years old now. I have a loving husband, whom I love. I have four wonderful children, all educated (including one at Oxford University, England). I have a lovely home.

I was well protected. But the hurt is still there, and it will always be there. I love my sons, and nothing else matters. It is definitely time to stop the madness. I very often think of my Bob, in his grave at twenty years old. I think of how he died, not in a comfortable bed, not with his loved ones around, but in torment. At one time back then, I thought of doing away with myself, but I knew it would hurt my parents too much.

One time, when one of my sons was being married, all of my children were on the altar for the ceremony, and I thought to myself, "Well, Bob, see our family? We've done well." My family is his family, because he is and always will be a part of me.

As I sit here thinking, I remember our wedding rings, a matching set. His ring was the one thing I wanted back and never did get. I was told that the North Koreans most likely took it off his body. I did get back many boxes I had sent him, undelivered and in very bad shape. I used to write to Bob twice a day, once on my break at work and once at night in my bedroom. I would write pages and pages of everything. He never told me he was in the fighting zone; he always said everything was all right and I was not to worry. When the news came, I was totally devastated.

We had two songs that were our favorites, "Oh, Happy Day," and "Smile, Sweetheart, Smile." I have records of the two, but I still cannot listen to them.

After forty years, the facts sometimes become dim, but never the hurt.

LEE R. DENNIS

I first went into the service on September 18, 1946. I joined the Army Air Forces for three years. After basic training, I went to Signal Supply School, and then I went overseas. I was assigned to the Fifth Air Force as a signal supply clerk in Japan. I got out of the service in June 1949, but in January 1950 I decided to go back into the service. I liked Japan, and I wanted to go back. There were no air force vacancies anywhere in Japan, but I was told I could get there by enlisting directly into one of the three U.S. Army infantry divisions based there. I chose the 24th Infantry Division because it was in the southern islands. I thought that would be a good place to spend the summer months. Also, I didn't think it would get very cold in the winter months. I didn't really like the idea of being in the infantry.

After I got to Japan, I was assigned to Headquarters Company, 24th Infantry Division, which was based on the island of Kyushu. After getting used to the climate, I began living it up in the nice, warm sunshine on the beaches. The infantry didn't seem so bad after all.

Then all hell broke loose on June 25, 1950. My sunshine beach parties ended. The 24th Infantry Division was the first U.S. Army unit into the Korean War (pardon me, *police action!*).

I was with the advance party of Headquarters Company, 24th Infantry Division. We would go as far ahead of the main body of Headquarters Company as possible to support and relay orders to and from the commanders on the front. Even though we were in the division headquarters company, we would always advance right behind the frontline troops. At night, we could always see and hear much of the action taking place on the front.

In summer of 1950, I was a witness at the scene of the Taejon massacre. That is the place where the 34th Infantry Regiment of the 24th Infantry Division was overrun on July 20, 1950, and Major General William F. Dean, the division commander, was captured.

Seeing the scene of the massacre is something I will never forget. There had been a great number of bodies scattered all over the Taejon area, so the townspeople had picked them all up and put them all in one location, for identification

purposes. Since the Korean conflict was called a "police action," you could caption my photo of the bodies, "Here lay
some dead policemen."

I don't believe there are any American troops in this group
of bodies; I think these are only ROK soldiers. I'm pretty
sure the American bodies had already been removed from
the area before we arrived there. The smell was so bad that
we could hardly breathe without something over our noses.
The soldier in the photograph removed the handkerchief from
his face only so I could take the picture. There were many
horrible scenes in the Taejon area. One real horrible one was
an ROK soldier buried in a hole up to his neck with a bayo-
net through his head.

For a long time after I saw all this, I had bad nightmares.
I would wake up shaking all over. The doctor said I would
probably overcome it with time.

DR. L. VALENTIN FEYNS

I am a refugee from Romania, a country that shared with
North Korea the dubious honor of running the most inhu-
man form of Communism.

We came to the United States in 1976, after twenty-four
years of unsuccessful attempts to emigrate. Our story isn't
as dramatic as Dr. Chung's, but we had our share of persecu-
tions, fear, and struggle. We also were fortunate to be a given
a chance to share in the opportunities of this blessed land.
For myself, a chemist, the opportunity was a fellowship at
the National Cancer Institute. Today, I am a supervisor in
the Drug Research and Testing Laboratory of the United
States Pharmacopia. My wife runs her own bookkeeping business. Our older daughter graduated *summa cum laude* from
Princeton University, and our younger daughter earned her
degree at Lehigh University.

With what I think to be a deep understanding of Dr.
Chung's accomplishments and feelings, I salute him. I salute

Donald Book

Jim Costa

George Culp

William Funchess

Luke Kim

Melba Lawson, with
Barbara, at the funeral
of Robert Lawson.
(Melba Garrow)

June and Robert Lagess. (Ruth DeBlois)

Earl Knier

The O'Connor family, 1958.

Harold Pedersen

Sergeant Chapman Spencer. Killed in action, April 1953

Sal Spinicchia

Ernest Williams and Johnny

him not only for what he has achieved as a professional and as a human being, but for his dedication to the double obligation that we have: the obligation to tell the story so that it will not be forgotten, and the obligation to pay at least partly the immense debt of gratitude that we have.

WILLIAM FUNCHESS

I spent thirty-eight months in Korea during the war—four months as an infantry officer with the 24th Infantry Division and then thirty-four months as a POW in North Korea. I was captured by Chinese Communists near Anju, North Korea, on November 4, 1950, and spent most of my time in POW camps near the Yalu River, at Pyok-tong and Pin-Chon-Ni. I was befriended by older North Korean civilians on several occasions while I was a POW but, generally, the POW ordeal in North Korea was a horrible experience. While in captivity near the Yalu, I was touched by the terrible plight of many of the poor North Korean children and civilians.

I probably owe my life to a South Korean civilian named Chon. He approached me in an apple orchard near Taegu in the summer of 1950 and asked to join my unit. He wanted to carry a rifle. We finally agreed to let him accompany us if he would serve as a medic or first-aid man rather than as a combat soldier. Chon, about twenty Americans, and I were captured on November 4. I was shot in the foot and could hardly walk, but on the long march north, Chon would somehow get a blanket for me each day when we stopped marching. The guards would usually take the blanket away once they saw it. We reached a temporary camp near Thanksgiving 1950, and I never saw or heard from Chon again. I don't know if he is dead or alive, and I do not know how to get any information on him. Although I will never see or hear from him again, I will forever be indebted to him.

Life as a prisoner of war in North Korea was, at best, a miserable experience. The winters were bitterly cold, and many of us spent the first winter in unheated mud shacks near the Yalu River, clad only in the summer uniforms that we wore when captured. Neither the Chinese who captured us nor the North Koreans provided any additional clothing or blankets the first winter. We were so crowded that we slept "spoon-fashion" on the mud floors, and the torn rice-paper windows allowed cold air to rip at our bodies. Men often suffered frostbite, and some even froze to death inside the small, cold rooms.

It was only a couple of weeks after capture that we became aware of an itching sensation and then of little creatures crawling in the hair on the back of our necks. Close inspection revealed lice—dozens of them on each of our bodies. They were white, about a quarter inch long, and they laid hundreds of tiny yellow eggs in the seams of our shirts and pants. Those of us who had the energy and hopes of survival spent a couple of hours each day taking off one piece of clothing at a time and popping the lice between our fingernails. Then we would seek out the eggs and pop them, too. Those POWs who were too sick or despondent just left the lice alone and let them suck. The heavily infested POWs would eventually turn ash gray color and then often died within forty-eight hours.

Our ration for the first several months consisted of millet seed boiled in melted snow—one cupful in the morning and another at night. There was no meat, no salt, no vegetables, and very little taste. It wasn't enough to sustain human life too long. We had hunger pains twenty-four hours a day and suffered from bone aches, sore mouths, night blindness, sensitivity to sunlight, diarrhea, and other ailments. I had no way of telling how much I weighed that first winter, but I feel that it was less than one hundred pounds. We POWs were a strange sight: ribs showing, legs and arms like toothpicks, little necks that you could almost reach around with one hand.

Winter temperatures along the Yalu River usually stayed ten to thirty degrees below zero, causing everything to freeze and stay frozen. There was no water, none to bathe with and none to drink. The winter of 1950—1951 we quenched our thirst with snow off the ground and then suffered from stomach cramps. I did not have a drop of water to drink from November 4, the day that I was captured, until February 1951, when a captured Catholic chaplain melted some snow in a makeshift pan over a corn stalk fire and gave me a few sips of warm water.

The machine-gun bullet that hit me just before capture tore through my foot, taking flesh and bone with it. The only medical treatment that I ever received for my wound was one bloody bandage that had been discarded by a wounded Communist soldier. Every step that I took for the next four or five months was pure torture. I am still amazed that I survived the three-week march over frozen mountain roads to the POW camp.

Then came hepatitis. I don't know where I caught it, but conditions were so unsanitary that many POWs came down with the ailment. Some survived it, some didn't.

Medicine? There was none whatsoever. I lost my appetite and just stopped eating. Some of my platoon members in another compound heard about my condition and sent me several hot peppers, two cloves of garlic, and a small brass spoon that they had scrounged. One of the men in my room crushed the peppers and garlic, sprinkled some on top of my cup of millet, placed my head in his lap, and fed me like a baby. After several days of spoon-feeding, the supply of peppers and garlic was exhausted, but by this time I had gained enough strength to feed myself. And then the hunger pains returned.

The "brainwashing" sessions began several months after I was captured. The Communists would take us outside in the bitter cold, set up guards and guns to keep our attention, and lecture us all day long. First it was in Chinese and then translated into broken English which caused the sessions to be doubly long. They read us *The Communist Manifesto,* the writings and works of Marx, Engels, and Lenin, as well as a book entitled *The Twilight of World Capitalism* by an American Communist named William Z. Foster. They tried to convince us that South Korea started the war by invading North Korea, that the American system of free enterprise was doomed to failure, that the U.S. Air Force was guilty of bacteriological warfare, that the Chinese soldiers in Korea were volunteers, that black was white, and a lot of other hogwash that was impossible to accept.

At night they came into our dark rooms with flashlights and made us take turns describing our "cognition" of the day's session. I had trouble with this since my physical and emotional condition prevented my comprehending much of the day's lecture. I was aware of this shortcoming but could do nothing about it. And to tell the truth, I really didn't try too hard.

Although the brainwashing sessions lasted throughout our captivity, they certainly were not effective. There were no "believers" in my camp.

I have no accurate count, but I believe that 60 to 70 percent of the American POWs in Camp 5 at Pyok-tong died during the winter of 1950—51. I would occasionally hobble down to the enlisted-men's compound, where I saw frozen bodies of the dead stacked in the snow like cordwood. The stacks were twenty or thirty yards long and three or four feet high. There were always several such stacks that first winter.

Every week or ten days, all the able-bodied men would have to fall out for burial detail. The frozen bodies were carried about a half mile out of camp and placed in the snow just above the water level of the reservoir on the Yalu River. The Americans on the burial detail placed a dog tag in the mouth of each dead man and retained the other tag so that it could later be turned over to U.S. authorities. It was a noble effort, but it was all in vain. The Communists removed the tags from the bodies and then confiscated the other tags. They deliberatly prevented us from maintaining any accurate records of those who died at the hands of the Communists.

We could later see dogs and vultures feeding on the remains of the dead, and when the thaws came in the spring of 1951, many of the bodies were washed into the reservoir and were lost forever in the chilly waters of the Yalu River.

One of the small rooms that I occupied that first winter held twelve men. Sometimes we would go a week or two with no deaths in the room, while other times we would lose several during the week. As a person died the Communists would immediately move in another to take his place. One morning, I tried to awaken the man on my left, but he had died during the night. Then I tried to awaken the man on my right, and blood gushed from his mouth as I moved him. He, too, was dead. Many were the times as I found my place on the floor before darkness that I asked aloud, "I wonder if I will see the sun rise tomorrow?"

The winter of 1950—51 was the most horrible experience that the mind can possibly visualize. It is hard to conceive that human beings could be so cruel and inhumane to their fellow man. It is almost impossible to believe that captured American military men were subjected to such pain and barbaric treatment. But it happened. It happened up there in Camp 5 on the Yalu. Is it any wonder that many of the Korean ex-POWs still relive the experiences and still suffer from bone-chilling nightmares?

Sometime in May 1951, the frozen waters of the Yalu melted and I had my first bath in six months. In the summer of 1951 we received some wheat flour that we mixed with water, rolled the dough thin with sticks, cut it into strips that we hung on the barbed wire to dry, and then boiled our crude "noodles" in water. What a wonderful improvement over millet seed! That summer we also received some vegetables, some soybeans, a small taste of pork, some salt, a white shirt, a thin blue jacket, blue pants, and a blue cap. We even got a two-foot square of cloth that the Chinese guards said we could fashion into socks. Things were looking up! By this time most of the deaths had stopped and many of us had even gained a few pounds.

I spent my second and third winters at Camp 2, which was seven or eight miles upriver from Pyok-tong. There we were housed in an old school building. The Communists installed some heaters in the hallway that were made from twenty-five- or thirty-gallon drums. The stovepipes ran overhead through our rooms and that was our sole source of heat. We continued sleeping on the floor, but now each man had an area that was about two feet by six feet. We were each issued a thin blanket, a cheap cotton comforter, and a cotton padded uniform, but the only way to stay even remotely warm was to huddle up just as close as possible to the man beside you.

The brainwashing sessions continued, and I had several rather serious run-ins with my captors. It came to a head one night when I was caught encouraging the others to make noise in a display of protest over our treatment. I spent the next thirteen days in a hole in the ground, seven of which I shared with a Marine pilot who had been giving the Communists a hard time.

Another time I was taken away and placed in isolation for thirty days after the Chinese learned that I was one of three POWs who destroyed pictures and literature in their Communist library.

Another serious incident occurred during an outside brainwashing session, when the Chinese tried to claim that atrocities in the city of Anak, North Korea, had been committed by the U.S. Army. They displayed several large photos of a mass grave and of the dead. They claimed that this was "proof positive" that the U.S. Army was guilty. After a few minutes,

I stood and shouted, "It's a damned lie! Those atrocities were committed during a civil uprising by North Koreans against their fellow North Koreans!" When they asked how I knew this, I foolishly answered, "I was there!" That was a mistake, a big mistake.

At the war's end and after the sixty-day POW exchange had ended, I challenged the Chinese officers as to why I was still being held a prisoner. Their reply was, "You are not a POW." I then asked, "What am I if I am not a POW?" The response was, "You are a war criminal." Stunned by this, I then shouted, "What did I do to become a war criminal?" The Chinese reply was only two words, "Remember Anak."

Shortly afterward, with no explanation, I was loaded on the back of a truck with one armed guard. The ride lasted an hour or two, but not one word was spoken by either the guard or me. The truck finally stopped suddenly in a wilderness area. I just knew I was going to be shot. The English-speaking guard said, "Get off!" I slid off the back of the truck and stood wondering what was going to happen next. The guard then barked at me, "Walk down that path! If you step off the path you will be killed!" When I hesitated, he shouted, "Move!"

As I began walking down the narrow footpath, I placed my arms in front of my body in order to make as small a target as possible. Fortunately, nothing happened.

After I had walked several hundred yards, I spotted a parked vehicle up ahead that I soon recognized as a U.S. Army ambulance. The back doors were open, and I saw two people standing beside the doors. As I approached, a waiting American major said to me, "Lieutenant, you don't know how lucky you are to be here." I replied, "Yes, but what happened?" The major then told me that both sides were holding war criminals and, "Last night we agreed to release war criminals."

I felt my eyes becoming moist. This was the first time that I had shed tears since finally learning in the POW camp that my father had died seven months after my capture.

At the end of that narrow path I had just traveled in the Korean no-man's-land, my war, the forgotten war, had finally come to an end.

The shooting had stopped. The barbed-wire fences were gone. The brainwashing sessions had ended. The hunger pains were only a memory. But I soon learned that the after-effects of the war and POW imprisonment were still there.

I felt so lucky to have survived both the war and the POW experience. Surely the man upstairs looked out for me. I had finally returned to a loving wife and family. All my friends made me feel so welcome to be home again.

The army hospital at Fort Jackson operated on my foot and removed a mass of shattered bone where the machine gun bullet exited my foot. The big toe, however, had shortened and grew back crooked during my captivity. This affected my balance and made it painful to walk long distances. But at least my foot did not hurt anymore when I put on a pair of shoes. It felt like a toothache, however, when I did very much fast walking.

I got out of the army the day after I was discharged from the hospital. Six months later, I accepted a job as farm agent with the Clemson Extension Service. The job involved a lot of field work, and I began having trouble with my eyes. Glare from the sun was unbearable. I went to a local optometrist who told me that I needed sunglasses immediately. He walked out of his office, went to his automobile, and returned with his personal sunglasses, which he handed me. He was correct when he told me that I would probably need to protect my eyes from the glare of the sun for the rest of my life. His prognosis holds true some forty years later.

It wasn't too long after my return home before the jaundiced color of my skin had cleared and the after-effects of hepatitis seemingly disappeared. I lost three teeth as a POW, and another soon after my release. Some of my other teeth were badly decayed. I have lost count of the many trips that I made, and am still making, to the dentist.

My job as an extension agent soon made me realize that I was having trouble coping with difficult situations. Whenever I came under pressure, I suddenly came down with diarrhea. It was quite embarrassing at times. Medications seemed to help, but I have never been a person willing to rely on too many pills. Another problem that continues to give me trouble is a recurring numbness in my hands. I have been diagnosed as having several damaged vertebrae in my upper spine, and the doctors say this is the source of the problem. The only back injury that I can recall is when I fell down a frozen hillside on the march north shortly after my capture. It hurt a lot then, but I had to keep going. My family doctor prescribed traction when I was having back trouble nine years ago, and the treatment has proven effective. I still have the tendency, however, to drop small objects. Things like a fork or a pencil will often just drop from my fingers.

I had an unexpected heart attack at the age of fifty-six. There were no warning signs that I was able to detect. My cholesterol level and my blood pressure both seemed to be within acceptable levels. None of the doctors were able to explain why the attack occurred.

Like many other POWs, I have nightmares and sometimes wake up screaming. I seem to usually have two different dreams that happen over and over. One dream is that I am again surrounded by hundreds of the enemy; they are closing in on me, and I am helpless to prevent my capture. The other dream is that I am home on leave from the POW camp and must soon return. While at home, I am frantically collecting the bare necessities that every POW needs—toothbrush, comb, nail clippers, food, soap, razor, etc. Thank goodness the nightmares are now less frequent than they were several years ago. Another problem that I just can't seem to control: I doubt that a ten-minute period ever passes while awake that I don't think about the time I was a POW. It is very distracting to me, and I am careful to hide my thoughts from others for fear they will look upon me as some kind of psycho.

I find myself being a worrier. I worry not only about important matters but also about trivial things of little or no consequence. If I have a problem on my mind, I toss and tumble in bed at night. I tell myself to get a grip on things and this usually helps a little.

After my POW experience, I tended to be a loner. I felt uncomfortable in crowds—especially among strangers. My extension job, however, required me to come in contact with large numbers of people. I had to force myself to accept the crowds, the meetings, and the occasional talk that I had to present. I had to suffer the diarrhea that was sure to occur if I felt overwhelmed or made a goof in my presentation. Retirement from the job, as much as I loved the work, was my salvation.

Yes, I have scars from the Korean War as well as from the POW experience. The emotional scars, however, may be the deeper of the two. They certainly are more difficult to cope with.

MELBA GARROW

I was twenty-one years old, with a three-month-old daughter, when my husband, Sergeant Robert R. Lawson, was called from the inactive Army Reserves to the "police action" in Korea. On July 3, 1951, the day before my daughter's first birthday, he was killed in action. He was twenty-three. I was devastated. I could not understand why this should have happened to me and my child. We had lost a husband and father on foreign soil . . . for what?

At the time Robert went to Korea, I would have done anything to help. He wrote and asked if I could get a pistol for him. In his words, "Only the officers have pistols, and when the *Chinks* sneak up on us at night, I can't defend myself with a rifle." I knew of a man who collected pistols as a hobby, and he sold one to me. Though neither my mother nor I had ever handled a gun, we partially disassembled it and packed it into a three-pound coffee can. Fortunately, letters and packages to our soldiers were not censored. Later, Robert acknowledged receiving the pistol, which worked fine. It was a criminal act on my part, but I find it humorous today.

Radio station WSBT, is South Bend, Indiana, offered families of soldiers serving in Korea an opportunity to come to the station and record messages to their loved ones. My father-in-law and I sent a message along with those of many other families. I informed Robert of the broadcast. He wrote that he walked several miles to hear our voices, but for reasons unknown he missed us.

Three years after Robert's death, I found another wonderful man, and father. We now have five grown children. The oldest is Barbara Lawson Garrow.

DONALD G. HAYS

I am a veteran of the Korean War, the forgotten war. I was with the 4th Fighter-Interceptor Group, flying F-86s as cover for the B-29s coming up from Okinawa. At the time, I was very young and did not fully understand the significance of why the United Nations was involved, other than "we" were fighting the spread of Communism.

I lost some good friends over there, but we knew that that might happen. My best friend was a POW for nearly eighteen months and was one of the last to return over the Bridge of No Return.

We did our duty and came home. We got on with our lives. We did not feel that anyone owed us anything for a job that we did for our country. We only ask that the nation remember those who lost their lives in the "forgotten war" with a memorial.

I left the air force in August 1953, following President Eisenhower's orders for a reduction in force. That allowed me to attend college. I now have a Ph.D. and spent thirty-one years in the counseling field before retiring.

In 1976, I had the opportunity to return to Korea. This time I went as an educator to evaluate the high-school graduation programs offered to Eighth Army personnel stationed in Korea. My wife and I were able to visit the negotiations site at Panmunjom and witness the tenseness of the men from both sides who were stationed there. And to think that the negotiations were still going on so long after the cessation of the fighting.

DR. HYUN BONG-HAK

I have read many books about the Korean War, but none other has moved me as did *The Three Day Promise*. I read every line in all thirty-six chapters.

What caused me to be touched so deeply and caused me to shed so many tears? Is it because I, too, served in the ROK Army? Is it because I, too, escaped from Dr. Chung's home province in North Korea? These could be the reasons, along with others, that I was moved so deeply in my heart. But the real reason for my heartfelt and endless tears was the fact that, in spite of the inhumane and tragic war, Dr. Chung had a lasting love and sought a lasting truth. Dr. Chung worked hard to record the beauty of living.

Through thirty-three years, his mother's love protected him and guided him to become successful, and it inspired him to return to his homeland and reach his mother's grave, where he cried endlessly for wanting to see his mother again. After I read his book, I, too, cried before his mother's grave.

I hope that Dr. Chung's book will awaken the conscience of the political leaders of North Korea and South Korea, and that it will become a power that will help bring about the early reunification of Korea.

The Three Day Promise will become our people's—especially our Korean American people's—proud history. Even though it is an autobiographical record, it describes the strong purpose of the Korean people—a desire for justice, hard work, persistence, and unwavering spirit—which will help all of us to firmly establish our roots in the United States. And it will help other Americans to understand us.

The Three Day Promise is a book that our second-generation Korean Americans must read.

GLEN E. JOHNSON

During the Korean War, I served as a U.S. Army counter-intelligence agent. While most of my duties were in Japan, I traveled to Seoul and Inchon immediately after the truce, and I had occasion to observe some of the country. What struck me the most was that every building, tree, post, or whatever was riddled with bullet holes. It was almost inconceivable that so many bullets could be fired, and I wondered as my jeep rolled through the countryside how the people would ever possibly rebuild their lives and cities.

During a war, most soldiers give little thought to the fact that the enemy is a person much like themselves. He has a family, wife, sweetheart, career, and other similarities. It would be good if many Korean War veterans would read Dr. Chung's book and reflect back on their memories of that sad conflict that seems not to be finished, even to this day.

JIU KIM

I am a young schoolgirl, and I only know about the north through our studies of history and geography. I always thought that North Korea was a faraway place. It is closest to us, yet it is far away from us because we cannot go there. After I read *The Three Day Promise*, I realized that the North Koreans are our own people, with the same blood. It is my sincere hope that Korea will be united soon, so we can share our lives together.

DR. LUKE I. C. KIM

I have just finished reading your book, *The Three Day Promise*. Your heroic story of courage and determination is truly inspiring. I am awestruck by your poignant life story, the eternal love of your mother, and the fact that you could not fulfill seeing your mother before she passed away.

Your life story, in some ways, parallels mine, although I did not go through as many hardships and dangerous situations as you did. I also came down to the south from North Korea (Shinuiju) and went through the Korean War, medical school, and the vicissitudes of internship and residency in psychiatry in the United States, which I also have made my home.

I was discharged from the Republic of Korea Navy in 1952 and allowed to complete my medical education at the Seoul National University School of Medicine. During the long summer vacation from the university in 1953, I was fortunate to be employed as a secretary and interpreter for the International Red Cross stationed at Panmunjom, the so-called "Peace Village" near the 38th Parallel.

During armistice negotiation meetings, I had the privilege of sitting in and observing the negotiations occasionally as a secretary to the International Red Cross team. While working at the Red Cross, I made attempts through their channels to find out about my mother—whether she is still alive and her whereabouts—but to no avail.

At times, there were silly but symbolically serious tactics displayed during the armistice negotiation meetings. For example, while arranging the room and getting ready for a meeting, the Communist-side person would inconspicuously make the extendible Communist flagstand on the table slightly taller than the U.N. flag. Recognizing this, the U.N.

personnel would then make the U.N. flag slightly taller than the Communist flag. And so forth. Both sides kept outdoing one other in tandem, raising the height of the flags until both were displayed in obviously very high standing positions on the table. Representatives of both sides chuckled openly. My overall impression of the cease-fire negotiation meetings was that the Communist delegates were much more aggressive, and manipulative, and took more initiative in setting up agendas or making proposals than U.N. delegates.

One of the items agreed on in a negotiation meeting was to set up a telephone hotline between the Communist command and the U.N. command for any emergency communication. For a while, an American sergeant and I were assigned to the post where the hotline telephone was set up. The sergeant and I slept in the army cots, waiting for telephone calls from the Communist command. We had only one or two calls over the period of two or three weeks. We were bored and had a lot of time to kill. The sergeant spent most of his time playing solitaire, and I spent time reading.

After the cease-fire was agreed on and the repatriation of prisoners was in progress, our International Red Cross teams were stationed at the repatriation inspection stations, one in the Communist zone and the other in the South Korean zone of the 38th Parallel. The role and duty of the Red Cross team was to inspect and supervise the prisoner-exchange process of the repatriation. I was assigned to the Red Cross inspection station to supervise the repatriation taking place in the Communist zone. I functioned there as an interpreter.

As truckloads of North Korean soldiers were brought in to the exchange station from the south, the men waved their fists and shouted. "Down with Yankees!" They also sang their military songs and threw away their newly issued green U.N.-supplied military fatigues and shoes. By the time they were out of sight, most of the Communist prisoners were almost naked, except for their shorts. Many shouted, "These dirty Yankee clothes; we don't need them." I found it interesting that they threw away these clothes only after the trucks had driven into the Communist zone. The road was cluttered with many discarded military fatigues and shoes, but when we returned to the same site the following day, all the new clothes and shoes had been picked by North Korean soldiers.

When the North Korean and Chinese prisoners were turned over to the Communist receiving officer, they went through a brief ritual. The officer would stand straight at attention and salute the returning prisoners while loudly reciting, "Welcome, our comrades; I welcome you to the bosom of our fatherland." Then the prisoners would respond in shouting voices: "*Mansei* [long life] to the People's Republic of Korea! *Mansei* to our great leader, Kim Il-sung!" They appeared to be well nourished and in high spirits.

In contrast, when the American prisoners were turned over to the U.S. military receiving officers, many of them appeared tired, but in a quiet, happy mood. Some, however, were somber or sobbing. I overheard an American war correspondent asking an American prisoner how he was doing and what he wanted to know most about what was going on in the United States at the time. The soldier asked him, "How is Marilyn Monroe doing these days?" Another soldier asked, "What's the score of the New York Yankees game?" I thought to myself, What a difference! Obviously, the Communist prisoners were completely indoctrinated and had been instructed to shout and protest vigorously like angry political animals, while American prisoners behaved as simple human beings who were in pain.

While we were observing and supervising the exchange process, the Communist prisoners formed a long line outside the Red Cross inspection-station tent. They wanted to talk to our Red Cross team, one at a time, to lodge complaints verbally or in written papers to our International Red Cross representatives from the United States, Denmark, Australia, the Philippines, and England, regarding how inhumanely they had been treated by the American guards while they were incarcerated in prisoner-of-war camps. They wanted to show the Red Cross representatives any signs of their physical malaise, scars, malnutrition, and so on as evidence of inhumane treatment they received. They insisted that the Red Cross team carefully document their complaints and the evidence of cruelty they presented.

In a subsequent joint meeting of the Red Cross representatives of both sides, the Communist delegates proposed that, based on what they heard and saw, the Red Cross supervising team should declare to the whole world that it had found the evidence of inhumane treatment and cruelty their prisoners had suffered at the hands of the U.N. guards. The Red Cross representatives of the U.N. side more or less walked out of the meeting.

DR. SUNG-HOU KIM

I was born and grew up in Taegu, and I experienced the Korean War while I was in Taegu as a middle-school student.

Ideological differences among different parts of the world are gradually diminishing, and hopefully so is human misery and tragedy brought about by these differences. This general trend may bring about the reunification of North and South Korea sometime in the future. As a Korean American scientist living in the United States, I feel I would like to participate in such a movement nonpolitically.

EARL KNIER

On February 3, 1950, I turned eighteen and enlisted in the U.S.Marine Corps. I went to Parris Island, South Carolina. Little did I realize then that in the fall I would be in the Land of the Morning Calm, landing at Wolmi-do, at Inchon, and fighting my way up through Seoul, the Chosin

Reservoir, Hungnam, Pusan, Masan, and other places until August 1951.

I sustained superficial wounds on July 15, 1951, while serving with Love Battery, 4th Battalion, 11th Marines. I was hurt by a 76mm shell in a place called Shrapnel Valley. We lost one of our guns there, and had another gun damaged. They had us zeroed in pretty well in that whole valley.

In August, I came home on a point system. Over here, I heard nothing about Korea. I still had friends over there, but I couldn't get any news, and I couldn't find any peace. Finally, I reenlisted in the Marine Corps so I could go back. I had a year left on my first enlistment, and I could pick my own duty station by reenlisting. So I picked Korea. That should have told me I was crazy, then and there.

I was with Antitank Company, 1st Marine Regiment, when they secured the shooting on-line on July 27, 1953. I was on the main line of resistance that night. They threw up flares, and we threw up flares. And they invited us over to a party. They had record players playing, and girls, and dancing, but we didn't go over.

I was happy that night, but I was sad, too, because of all the wasted lives, and what the war had done to the Korean civilians as well.

I've always been as Hawk-Dove. I like to think of it as being warrior. I detest war, and I detest and hate people who would think of starting one. But I believe we need professionals, and we need to stand for what is right, and for freedom. We need to put down wrong, and to stand in the gap for others when they're not able to stand for themselves. This is how I felt about Korea. I love that land.

I had a chance to go back to Korea in 1993, but I couldn't because I'm on oxygen at all times–I have emphysema–and there were too many ifs about whether my needs could be met at all times in Korea. I would have loved the chance to go back. I still visualize the good things I saw in Korea, the beauty.

◆

In 1987, my son was a wrestler for Notre Dame High School, here in Batavia, New York. He's a nice-looking young man, a muscular, all-American boy. He didn't do drugs, or anything like that. He wanted to be like his dad and join the service. He finally decided on the navy. I tried to talk him out of it, but his mind was set, so I gave my blessing. But all I could think of, as I looked at him after that, was what I had done in Korea, what I had seen, and what I and others had been through there. I couldn't handle it.

I ended up in the psych ward at the VA hospital in Buffalo. I had an extended stay. That's where they diagnosed me as having a nervous condition they call post-traumatic stress disorder–PTSD. They wanted me to put in a claim, but I was in denial; I couldn't do that. I'm a professional Marine; I couldn't admit I had a problem. And that's where my life was when Donald Chung's book came to my attention. I was at an all-time low because I was seriously thinking about trying to stop things, and get off.

One day in December 1989, I was reading "Dear Abby" and I saw that a Korean fellow was offering his book, *The Three Day Promise*. I was deeply touched by what I read, so I wrote Dr. Chung for the book. I was very unstable at that time, still suffering from the PTSD. But I was still in denial and didn't think I had such a thing. I always knew that there was something wrong with me, but I couldn't quite lay my finger on it. I thought maybe I was just wild, or couldn't settle down. I knew I was certainly different than the rest. So I wrote Donald, and I got the book. I was deeply touched as I read the book.

Donald Chung called me on Christmas Day, 1989. There were just my wife and I here. I was so touched to hear his voice on the other end of the line. Emotionally, I broke down. I couldn't handle it. I cried. I was so overwhelmed with this man's love, and his sincerity. He cried with me. Finally, I handed the phone to my wife; I just couldn't speak. I was so grateful, and I have been ever since, that he felt that much about me, that he called.

I ended up in the VA hospital again in January 1990—a few weeks after Dr. Chung called—with a respiratory problem. Rumors were that they were going to start a stress program next door to my ward. I was put in contact with a doctor who, when he came to see me, decided to counsel me right away if I was willing to participate. I did. In April, we started a group of Korean War veterans that I still attend today.

We have four guys who were POWs for three years, and other men who were there at various times. We've grown quite a bond of friendship; we support one another. And I now have an upgraded disability, which is a blessing to my wife, who suffered for so many years. I can't say enough for the program coordinator at the PTSD Clinic, Roger Hines, who is a veteran of the Vietnam War.

I am receiving the help I need. It doesn't mean I'm cured, but I'm much better off today than I was when Donald Chung called me. I'm happier, and I'm able to enjoy a few things. I went to a Chosin Few reunion in New Orleans a few years ago, in my wheelchair, with my oxygen. I met friends there I hadn't seen in forty-plus years. It was great! I even danced on the floor in my wheelchair. I had a good time, and my wife did too. I was grateful that I was able to go there. It was a highlight of my life.

Thank God for being alive.

YOON-HEE LEE

Since I was born in 1959 and my husband in 1957, both of us did not experience the painful Korean War tragedy.

We Koreans have forgotten our past, and sometimes we cover up our past while we are busy making a living. What makes it more painful is that our generation has taken its good life for granted. We have not tried to understand the painful lives our parents' generation lived during the Korean War. Today, our generation and our children's generation can live happily and can dream big dreams. But *The Three Day Promise* made me realize that the happiness and dreams would not have been possible without the willingness of our parents' generation to sacrifice their very lives.

Why did so many young people have to die or be wounded, and why were so many thousands of people separated from their loved ones in a war among our own people? Whenever I think of the tragedies of the Korean War, it makes me so sad and sick. Dr. Chung's clear description of the Korean War, his painful separation from his family, and even his successful life in America represents the pains our people endured because of the war. Through Dr. Chung's book, I have felt many of the pains he experienced, my heart was aching, and I cried many times. Even though my parents are not separated from their families and my relatives did not experience those pains, my heart still hurt and I was saddened by the Korean War tragedies. I will never be able to forget.

Since reading *The Three Day Promise,* I have been more appreciative of the war generation, which has been poor and sick, and lived such difficult lives in the midst of the fighting. Perhaps it is true that people forget the tragedies of war one by one, but those of us who have clear sense will never forget the sacrifice of those who gave their lives and a painful past for our people. Through our remembrances of those tragedies of the war, we must not be discouraged. Rather, we must find purpose in life itself and attempt to live our own lives properly. Through the enduring memory of my generation and future generations, the sacrifice and the drive for success—the contribution of the war generation—will not have been in vain.

As a common citizen of Korea, I wish to challenge every Korean to work and pray toward the unification of our people and our land.

LEONORE T. MAHOWALD

My husband, Robert, is a West Point graduate. We were newly married and stationed in Japan when the Korean War started. We served with the 35th Infantry Regiment, 25th Infantry Division, from July 1950 to August 1951.

Several years ago, we went to Korea to visit. Such a beautiful country. When we were landing at Kimpo, my husband looked out of the window and said, "The last time I was at Kimpo, I was driving across the airfield under fire, and my driver was killed." It was all quite an experience for him.

JESS R. McELROY

I was in World War II as a gunner in torpedo bombers, got out of the service, and finished high school. When the Korean War started, I was called back to active duty as an aircrewman flying all-weather and night attack mission in AD-4Ns off the USS *Valley Forge*. I was shot down over North Korea in 1951, and I spent twenty-one months as a guest of both the North Koreans (in Pyongyang) and the Chinese (at Camp 2 in Pi-Chongni).

After the war, I decided to stay in the navy, and I retired in 1967. The government then hired me back as a civilian, and I helped train 42,000 naval aviators and other high-risk personnel in SERE (survival, evasion, resistance, and escape). As a result of my experience as a prisoner and a trainer, I believe that so-called collaborators in the Korean and Vietnam wars got a raw deal. They had no training in what they were going up against.

World War II vets came back and went to school and got jobs. We had problems, but we didn't cry about it, even when vets made headlines for doing something wrong. Korean War vets came back to the McCarthy era, the Doolittle Commission, yellow journalism, investigations, and more.

We still don't have a memorial. The money is available, but in-house fighting and others problems have arisen. We do have a meditation bench and Koran pine tree at Arlington Cemetery that were donated by the Korean government, which I guess is better than nothing.

It's not the Congress or the Pentagon that wins wars. They are hindrances, and in some cases they give comfort to the other side. It's the kids out of school and off farms, etc., who go in and do the job. They are still doing it, and they will do it in the future.

TONY NOLLET

I spent fourteen months in Korea, just after the armistice was signed. I flew Marine Corps fighters out of K-6 Airfield. We had a few days of excitement when Chinese MiGs decided to overfly South Korea, and I had a lot of fun shooting pheasants and flying the airplanes. Alas, I did not get to know the Korean people as I should have done.

Our squadron had adopted an orphanage located close to K-6, and I visited it every few weeks, armed with a ten-pound tin of hard candy that my uncle shipped to me from Minnesota. At the orphanage I met a marvelous four-year-old girl. She was about the cutest human being I ever met, and she proved to be the brightest. We couldn't communicate orally, so I turned to mathematics. When I wrote $2+2=$ she immediately wrote 4. I continued with more difficult problems and found that she could perform long division accurately. Thanks to help from my grandmother, I too had mastered long division at age four, but I had never before found anyone so young who could duplicate the feat. Then I tested her ability to extract the square root from long numbers. She performed flawlessly, and I knew that her natural intellect was superior to mine, as I had not learned to extract square roots until I was nine or ten.

The I made one of the biggest mistakes of my life. Had I used maximum effort, my wife and I could have adopted this magnificent child. But, thinking that my wife would reject the idea because we already had four children of our own, I didn't make the effort. Some years later, I discussed this with my wife and learned that she would have been delighted to adopt the little girl. I have wondered thousands of times whatever happened to "my" little girl. I have prayed thousands of times for her welfare. I hope that God has been good to her.

ERMA JEAN O'CONNOR

Korea and its people are very much a part of our lives. My husband, John, was there during the war, at Wonsan and Yonpo air bases, and Pusan, Chinhae, and Seoul. His last transfer during the war was to Seoul, where he served with the 1818th Air & Airways Communications Service (AACS) Wing as a pilot and communications officer. The unit headquarters was at Ewha College.

The Ewha College students had fled to Pusan at the war's outbreak and carried on their studies there. Dr. Helen Kim, president of Ewha at the time, became acquainted with John, and he served as her pilot, flying her from Pusan to Seoul on occasion to visit her campus and lecture American troops on Korean culture. During this period, there were many abandoned and orphaned Korean children forming into bands and raiding garbage cans on the military bases. The 1818th group commander appointed John as project officer with directions to find housing and care for these children. With the help of Korean military police, a large house was found, and what ultimately became the AACS Orphanage was born in 1951. About seventy-five children were given care. Very soon thereafter, AACS units worldwide eventually adopted the orphanage and supported the children until they all reached adulthood.

When John returned to the United States in 1953, he formed a group to unite hundreds of colleges and universities here for the purpose of securing scholarships and sponsorships for worthy Korean students.

In 1956, while our family—John, me, and our four children ranging in age from four to thirteen—was stationed in Japan with the U.S. Air Force, John made frequent flights to Korea to oversee the AACS Orphanage. During his trips from Japan, John enjoyed entertaining the children by playing Korean and American songs on his trumpet. It was from this orphanage in 1957 that we adopted Suh Kyung-ja (Helen) and Kim Soo-dong (James), then seven and eight years old, to join our four children. We also sponsored a Korean student who played the organ in the U.S. base chapel at Pusan, where John was based for a time. She is currently a professor of theater at a university in the United States.

Our oldest daughter, Polly, joined us when we flew to Korea to pick up Helen and James. Polly was invited to stay at the Ewha College dormitory with the college students, and John and I stayed at the orphanage. The commissary officer at our base in Japan packed up hot dogs, buns, and ice cream in dry ice as a surprise for the children at the orphanage. During our stay, John and Polly gave a trumpet-and-piano recital at Ewha College, and the proceeds were donated to the orphanage.

The following year, 1958, our whole family flew to Korea under the auspices of President Eisenhower's People to People Program. During this visit, John and our two daughters played with the Seoul Symphony Orchestra under the direction of John S. Kim. The family stayed at the home of Dr. Helen Kim, the Ewha College president.

After retiring from the air force in 1968, John joined the music department at the University of Illinois, and he was fortunate to be given two sabbatical leaves to Korea. His focus was on traditional music and dance, and he was successful in interesting the University of Illinois in developing a

Korean instrumental and dance studies program. The Korean government's Department of Culture donated an entire orchestra of traditional instruments along with furnishing teachers from Korea.

GAIL PARTAIN

Reading Dr. Chung's story in *The Three Day Promise* brought to my attention once again what I sometimes overlook–that I am fortunate to be an American. While as a nation we have our problems and corruptions, we enjoy the freedom to complain and try to make things better without having to suffer repression and the threat of death because we speak out.

I am thankful, too, that Dr. Chung is an American citizen now. I hope he never stops telling his story. It is only through hearing about what has happened and what can happen if we become complacent that we can avoid allowing our freedom to be taken away. We must be aware that good people have lost their freedom, and that it can happen within our shores.

I feel certain that Dr. Chung's family in North Korea is very proud of his achievements, especially in the face of such adversity. I am sorry that his mother was unable to share in his successes, but as a mother and grandmother myself, I do believe she knew well the character of the child she raised and felt in her heart that he would be well, no matter what.

HAROLD PEDERSEN

I was in the I U.S. Corps artillery, near Yonchon, in 1953. I did nothing heroic in Korea, and the tent I lived in was a luxury that many U.S. soldiers never had.

When I returned home in 1955, I noticed that my mother had left my shirt and trousers hanging on my bedpost, because she wanted it to seem that I had not left.

I follow with interest the news of unification talks in Korea. I feel that it is a tribute to those who died in the war that South Korea is so very successful. But it is still very sad that people should ever have to die for political reasons.

My thoughts about Korea (and all wars) as I approach old age and look back at the wonderful life I have experienced are about those on both sides of the conflict who died or were severely wounded. They were never able to fulfill their dreams or learn where life would otherwise have led them. That is the tragedy of war–cutting short lives of unique human beings, lives that would never again experience love and family, or have children or grandchildren, or see the many beautiful places on this Earth. So each "war" memorial is actually a "people" memorial, at which we can contemplate not only the loss of each person but the loss of the only chance each of those people had to experience the fullness of life, because diplomacy failed and the selfish goals of politics won.

EVA-CHUL SHIN

I am from the same generation as Dr. Donald Chung. To those who were born in North Korea and moved to South Korea, separated from their loved ones, *The Three Day Promise* spoke the feelings of our own experience. To those who were separated from their families, two things they cannot forget: "Good-bye" and "Reunion."

Dr. Chung meets the spirit of his mother. Many separated families will experience the same kind of meeting in the future. What should we learn from such meetings? We cannot just pass it by as a common experience. The Korean War was a war between the same people; the event is beyond our individual experience, it is our nation's experience. The mother who was waiting to see her own son within three days died without seeing him again. Imagine how anxiously she waited to see her son.

It is different to express the guilt the son felt because he was not able to keep his promise. This is the inseparable love between a son and a mother. This is where we can find the greatest authentic love and care that can be achieved by mankind: The anxiety of the mother waiting for her son who has left home, and the guilty feelings of the son who has returned too late.

Without any question, this tragedy was caused by the political and ideological differences of the North Koreans and South Koreans. Is a political difference more important than human love?

If we do not want more wars like the Korean War—if we do not want the tragedies of such a war—then we must think seriously about this dilemma. Why do we choose political and ideological goals while ignoring the genuine, natural love that exists between mothers and sons?

Those who hold politics and ideology above human love, and those who protect governments that do so, must accept the responsibility for such inhumane policies. They should think again on what is most important in life—political ideology or natural human love and caring.

Korea, unfortunately, has been separated for the past fifty years because of political and ideological differences. As long as one of the political systems ignores human love and caring, Korea cannot be reunited.

Who deserves the blame? The Communists must take the blame of the million human beings who became the victims of their selfishness, pride, and power. This blame is not leveled just by the separated families, but by the entire Korean people. The blame for Dr. Chung's mother not seeing her own son, even after waiting for so many years, should be that of the selfish political and ideological leaders.

♦

RICHARD A. SHOLTS

I was a member of the U.S. Air Force Communications Security unit in Korea in 1950 and 1951. I remember both sides of the roads lined with refugees as we moved from Taegu to Seoul and elsewhere.

I returned to Korea several times on business in the 1970s, and then I had an opportunity to return as a representative of Amoco Chemicals in a joint venture with the Samsung Group. I served in Korea for four and a half years as the executive vice president for the joint venture. While there, I studied the Korean language and culture very diligently. I later married a Korean lady, and we have a son.

In 1984, while serving as president of the American Chamber of Commerce in Korea, I wrote the following introduction to a Chamber publication entitled *Living in Korea:*

"Korea has been referred to as the "Hermit Kingdom" and the "Land of the Morning Calm." However, "The Land of the Continuing Economic Miracle" would perhaps be a more appropriate name these days. From the devastation of the Korean War and primarily an agricultural society, an economic miracle began to take root in 1962. Now, after [two decades] of rapid economic development, Korea has truly emerged as a newly industrialized country. . . . It is being studied as a model by many [less developed] countries around the world.

"A country with virtually no natural resources, and a society rich in Confucian tradition, Korea's economic development has truly been phenomenal. Its rapid growth rate has been the result of several interesting economic, political, and social factors. The commitment to industrialize, though dictated by circumstances, was successful, at least in part, because Korea has a very important resource: a well-educated, highly motivated, and industrious populace [which is] able to absorb and apply technology quickly."

BILL SIMPSON

I was drafted into the U.S. Army in May 1952 and assigned to the Signal Corps. I spent four months training in manual central office maintenance, a specialty I picked up because I figured there were no central offices on the front lines.

One week before Christmas 1952, we landed at Inchon. It took all night to unload three thousand of us. I boarded a train, which fortunately went south. I spent four months at the Hialeah Compound in Pusan, where were maintained the open-wire telephone lines to Ulson, forty miles to the north. Then I spent the next fourteen months at a long-line signal compound at Songdo Beach near Pusan. Our job was operating the Mukden cable, which ran from Mukden, Manchuria, to Tokyo.

Several yeas ago, I took part in a veterans' tour of Korea, for which the Korean government paid everything except the air fare. My wife and I began the trip three days early so we could spend some time in Pusan. Although I spent a whole day in the Songdo Beach area, I found nothing I recognized. *Nothing* I saw in Korea reminded me of my first time there.

The Korean government kept us busy with tours, formal dinners, etc. At our breakfasts, there was a microphone set up so members of the group could make comments. One of our group said that the first night, his body was still on U.S. time and he couldn't go back to sleep. So he got up, got dressed, and went for a walk. Our hotel was downtown and in walking distance to the train station. He came to an area of shopping stalls, and someone was selling music tapes. The American picked out a few and asked how much they were. The price was reasonable, but as he pulled out his wallet, the shopkeeper noticed an ID we had all been given that identified us as Korean War veterans. The shop owner refused to take any money for the tapes.

About the Korean people: There were two busloads of us, with a banner on each bus, telling who wewere. The kids were the friendliest. When they saw our buses, they waved and smiled. They ran up and practiced their English.

In China, the TV channel ran the same propaganda over and over: Be happy, run to your work, work hard, and be happy. Coming down from the Great Wall, I shared a tram car with three Chinese. One asked if I was from the United States. I said I was, and he said the United States is a great country. I thought that was kind of nice.

SAL SPINICCHIA

I served in Korea with the U.S. Marine Corps in 1951. I recently returned from a Revisit Korea tour sponsored by the Korean War Veterans' Association. After seeing firsthand the economic, industrial, and social progress the country has made, I feel that it was all worthwhile. I am proud to say that I played a small part in keeping your country free from Communist rule.

ERNEST R. WILLIAMS

In 1947 and 1948, I spent one year at Inchon and one year at Ascom City, not far from Kimpo. I visited most of the towns in the south, and most of the museums, and I tried to learn how to speak Korean. I even visited in the country and spoke with the farmers to learn their customs. At the end of 1948, I came back to the United States; I was glad to come home, but I hated to leave all my new friends. The thirty-eight Koreans who had been working for me put up their money and presented me with a gold diamond ring. They were poor and could not afford this gift, but that's the kind of friends they were.

When the war broke out in 1950, it almost broke my heart. I had just gotten married, and I told my wife I would be the first one to go because I was in a new company, the Mobile Combat Bakery. We were to follow the combat troops and bake fresh bread daily. We were issued all the combat gear, including machine guns. The company started out from Fort Bragg, North Carolina. We loaded our equipment on the train and then took a troop train to California, and then a ship to Korea. We docked one night at Pusan, Korea, about fifteen or twenty miles from the front line. They gave us each two bullets and an 18-inch machete knife. They said it was for the Korean jungles. I had been in Korea in 1947 and 1948, so I knew they did not have any jungles in Korea. We had guns but no bullets, so three of us visited the front lines to get some, and we almost got cut off by snipers. The enemy was pushing our troops back, closer to Pusan. We had ninety-nine men in our company, and half of them were taken to the front to fight.

In Pusan, thousands of people were pushed down from all over Korea, so many had no food or a place to live. A small boy, about five years old, was begging for food. I asked him his name, but he did not know. We went to my tent for food, and I tried to find out about him. It was then he told me that the enemy came in his house and shot everyone, and he ran out the back door. He did not know the area in which he lived or who did the shooting, had no knowledge of English, and knew very little of the Korean language. I told him he could stay with me, and I began to teach him English. He called me "father" in Korean, and I called him Johnny.

We moved to Inchon by ship and then followed the invasion force toward Seoul. Eventually, we were ordered to pick up the dead bodies of American soldiers. We drove around by the river and in Seoul, picking up the enemy dead as well as our own. Picking up bodies that were blown to pieces and living with the smell of decay contributed to the next six months of nightmares.

Within the next year, we moved around eighteen times. I took Johnny to Pyongyang in November 1950. I had to hide him because we could not take South Koreans past the 38th Parallel.

In Pyongyang, we moved into a badly damaged cigarette factory. We set up our bakery equipment and started to make bread, but before the bread was finished the Chinese came into town at night and made all sorts of noises. We were told we had twenty minutes to leave town or be surrounded. It was about thirty-eight degrees below zero that night. We took what we could and had to blow up the rest. We did not have time to load C rations, so we had no food for a few days. On the way out of town, shells were falling everywhere.

It took a long time to get to Seoul because the civilians filled the roads, walking and with carts and old trucks. When we got to Seoul, they told us to keep going south. When we stopped at Ascom City, we were told that we could not go south. We had to go back twenty miles to Yongdungpo in order to go south. It was snowing so hard we could not see. We were stopped to be given $10 of our pay at midnight that day. When asked why they did that, since there was no place to spend it, we were told it was for our morale. Days later, we were reunited with two of our missing trucks and four of our men and were told that an infantry division had kept them to help evacuate its men.

We stopped in Taegu a few days later. We had Christmas dinner with a field hospital. It did boost our morale to bathe and change clothes. We again set up to bake bread, but when we heard that the enemy took Seoul, we worried that our town would be next.

When headquarters found out I had a Korean boy with me in Taegu, they ordered me to "get rid of him." After I took Johnny to an orphanage in Taegu, he had returned twice. The hardest thing I ever had to do was to tell Johnny I did not love him–so he would stay at the home. I have not seen him since that day.

Then it was back to North Korea in the push back again across the 38th Parallel. We set up in Chungchong, and then I was sent home in February 1952.

When I was sent back to Seoul in 1959 and again in 1960, I checked out the orphanages, but I could never find Johnny.

I started giving shoes and clothing to the children of Korea when I was stationed there again in 1959 and 1960. I had asked my wife to send the clothing that no longer fit our two children, so I could give them to the Korean children who had nothing. I sent pictures back to my wife, showing how the children loved the clothes, and I even took some home movies of them receiving the clothing at the orphanages. My wife in turn gave the pictures to the town newspaper in Phoenixville, Pennsylvania, where they printed the story and my address in Korea so others could mail clothing. Soon people started leaving boxes and boxes of clothing on my door-step in Pennsylvania, as well as sending some directly to me in Korea. When the newspaper printed that it was hard for my family to pay for all the postage, some businesspeople dropped off some postage money. The story was also reprinted in the home states of our families, Texas and New York, which brought many more donations of clothing for the Korean orphans. It felt good to make so many children happy. The Korean government showed its appreciation for what I was doing by presenting me with a scroll citation and matching wedding bands for my wife and me.

STEVE CHONG-SOK YUN

I am a Korean American, a medical-school student. Both my parents were raised during the Korean War, and my mother, like Dr. Chung, was a North Korean refugee.

My father borrowed Dr. Chung's book from a friend, and then he gave it to me to read. Dr. Chung's story has given me great inspiration and insight. I hope to pass the book down to my children someday.

I cannot adequately express in words the impact and power *The Three Day Promise* has had on my thinking. I regard this book as a great treasure, and I look forward to sharing Dr. Chung's story with my friends and my future children.

EPILOGUE

Dr. Donald K. Chung still lives and works in Long Beach, California. The medical practice, which he continues to run alone, thrives despite his many time-consuming commitments relating to Korean War remembrances and bringing about the peaceful reunification of his homeland and people.

Thanks to Dr. Chung's generosity, all the money earned from sales of *The Three Day Promise* has been donated to the construction of the Korean War Veterans' Memorial in Washington, D.C. And all the money from the sale of *Remembrances of the Forgotten War* is being contributed to the Korea/Vietnam Memorial National Education Center in Bethlehem, Pennsylvania.

ACKNOWLEDGMENTS

I salute Abigail Van Buren for printing my letter about my autobiography and my intention to donate all proceeds from the book sales to the Korean War Veterans' Memorial Fund. The response from readers of twelve hundred daily newspapers to her December 1, 1989, column was overwhelming, and the fund-raising campaign became successful.

I also received many thousands of quite touching and deeply inspiring letters from Korean War veterans, survivors of veterans, Koreans who fought in the war, and young people who really know very little about the Korean War. I sincerely thank these readers for sharing their thoughts with me.

I especially wish to thank the following individuals who made my fund-raising campaign successful: the many volunteers who handled more than thirty thousand letters and checks, and who shipped the books; several local Korean book stores, for selling the book and donating the profits to the memorial fund; the Samsung Corporation for processing the mailing labels and underwriting a one-third-page ad in the

Central Daily newspaper for several months; Mr. Ron Yukelson, the director of public relations at Long Beach Memorial Hospital, for his sterling efforts to arrange interviews on the Voice of America, the Tom Snyder talk show, television stations KCBS and KNBC, twelve radio talk shows, and the American Medical Association periodical.

And I wish to thank Mr. Lance Colson, of Father & Son publishers, for prompt and timely service when printing additional copies of *The Three Day Promise*.

My boundless admiration for and thanks to the late General Dick Stilwell, chairman of the Korean War Veterans' Memorial Advisory Board, are for his tireless and energetic effort to see the construction of the memorial. He guided and encouraged me throughout my fund-raising campaign. I am sure that most Korean War veterans are deeply saddened for his death on December 25, 1991.

I also thank all the members of my office staff for their calm efficiency during mass confusion attending the arrival of mountains of letters. I was always able to carry on my professional service to all of my patients because of my staff's hard work.

Many thanks to each one of *The Three Day Promise* TV drama production team of KBS (Seoul), especially producer Mr. Lee Young-kook, screenplay writer Mr. Chung Hwa-young, and the actors and actresses who portrayed me and members of my family for their superb imitation. A total of fifty episodes of fifty minutes each aired June 1991 through November 1991. This was a most memorable experience for me and my family as well as many members of the Korean War generation living in South Korea and the Korean communities in America.

I thank my two sons for their great help and support, Richard, my elder son, took the adventurous (he thought) trip to North Korea with me in 1986 and expressed his views and feelings about life in Communist North Korea and the Korean War as a second-generation Korean American. And my younger son, Alexander, encouraged me and even insisted that I write *this* book.

I am also obliged to my editor, Mr. Eric Hammel, who gave me much valuable guidance for the outline of this new book and transformed it from my original manuscript to a readable text and finished product. He also interviewed and corresponded with many Korean War veterans and others whose stories appear as part of this book.

Finally, I thank my wife, Young-ja Chung, for the commonsense logic that made the all-important connection with Abigail Van Buren. Without her wholehearted support and the diary she kept every day, I could not have begun to write this book.

Chung Dong-Kyu
Donald K. Chung
Long Beach, California
1995